the
wandering
peacemaker

ROGER PLUNK

 HAMPTON ROADS
PUBLISHING COMPANY, INC.

the wandering peacemaker

Cover photograph and design by Mayapriya Long

For information write:

Hampton Roads Publishing Company, Inc.
1125 Stoney Ridge Road
Charlottesville, VA 22902

Or call: 804-296-2772
FAX: 804-296-5096

e-mail: hrpc@hrpub.com
Web site: www.hrpub.com

If you are unable to order this book from your local
bookseller, you may order directly from the publisher.
Quantity discounts for organizations are available.
Call 1-800-766-8009, toll-free.

Library of Congress Catalog Card Number: 99-091425

ISBN 1-57174-179-8

10 9 8 7 6 5 4 3 2 1

Printed on acid-free paper in the United States

To Azure, Leila, Gabriel and others
of the new generation.

CONTENTS

PREFACE

THIS SMALL BOOK is a telling of my experiences as an adviser and mediator in the political storms of Tibet, Kashmir, Burma, and Afghanistan. The common thread running through the stories is the dynamic relationship between government and spirituality. Because spirituality is a central theme, the book begins in part one with an exploration into the nature of spirituality and continues to touch on the subject in later chapters.

The classic work on this subject is Plato's *Republic*, which I read twenty years ago as a philosophy major. Occasional reference is made to Plato, but this is not a scholarly work. I do not draw from the authority of distinguished thinkers to build compelling arguments. I do not attempt to convince. I attempt only to share my reflections on my personal experiences, to share the light playing on the waters of my mind.

INTRODUCTION

IN JANUARY OF 1994 I had a private meeting with His Holiness the Dalai Lama at his home in Dharmsala, India. At that time, I was the constitutional adviser to his Constitution Redrafting Committee. The subject of the meeting was the constitutional relationship between Tibet and China.

The Dalai Lama is considered to be the incarnation of compassion. The full significance of this is not realized until one meets him. The defining aspect of his personality is the tremendous amount of love that flows from the man. It is incredible. I had no expectations about him. But when he put his gaze on me and smiled, I felt hit by a large wave of love. To have an intelligent conversation with him, I had to regain my senses and really focus under the scrutiny of his sparkling eyes.

The Dalai Lama has an exceptionally sharp mind. And because he spends much of his time (outside of prayer and meditation) talking to guests from every level of our global society, he also is well informed. I brought up the issue of an autonomous Tibet inside China. An autonomous region is an area within a country that has its own govern-ment and decides issues of local character, leaving the national issues to the national government. All states in the

United States have a certain amount of autonomy. The Dalai Lama looked at me and said, "Autonomy has been our policy for fifteen years." Then he paused and said, "But some Tibetans do not like the idea," and he threw back his head and laughed that deep belly laugh of his. He was really amused by it.

I suggested that a constitution for an autonomous Tibet would therefore be more suitable than one for independence (which is what his committee had me drafting). He was now wide-eyed and surprised and said, "You mean you're not doing a constitution for an autonomous Tibet? The chairman of the committee knows our policy is for autonomy. It should definitely be done." Then he directed his secretary to make the necessary arrangements. When the meeting was over, he held me with both arms in loving embrace, as he walked me out to the patio to say good-bye. While he was leading me out, all I could think was that I was being held by a sparkling beam of love.

I soon discovered by direct experience that there was strong resistance against the idea of autonomy within the Dalai Lama's administration. Many officials remained strong advocates of Tibetan independence. The autonomy issue was therefore sizzling hot, and no one wanted to touch it. There was a conflict in policy among the Tibetans, and I stepped right in the middle of it.

This was typical of my experiences as a mediator in Asia. Disputes were never just between two parties, such as the Dalai Lama and China's Jiang Zemin, who needed reconciling. A vast play of conflicting forces between individuals, and between groups of people within groups of people, was always involved. They wove a great web of complexity that boggled the mind. Yet in looking for solutions, I always gravitated back to simplicity. The reason for this was that solutions are invariably spiritual in nature: breaking old ways of thinking, appealing to the noble and sacred in people, and transforming hate into love and bigotry into compassion.

The reason the Israeli-Palestinian peace process has been so difficult to resolve is that the obstacles to peace are rigid thinking, deep-rooted hatreds, and emotional injuries. From an academic point of view, establishing a Palestinian state is the obvious answer for peace. But in reality, the process of doing so involves a type of spiritual healing of the people to overcome their deep suspicions, fears, prejudices, and hatreds. Spiritual healing is a simple concept. But implementing such healing is a difficult and challenging task.

Another simple observation I have made is that international events are increasingly in the hands of people, not just governments. A global democratization is going on that transcends national borders. It is, after all, the people's world. Business people, housewives, writers, artists, academics, and the countless nongovernment organizations (NGOs), such as the International Red Cross and *Medicenes Sans Frontiers* (Doctor's Without Borders), are invariably at the forefront of change. Governments are often pushed forward by them or dragged behind them. A recent example—a tip of the iceberg—is the International Treaty to Ban Land Mines, initiated by a small NGO.

My own story is a testimony to the value of the private sector in international affairs. I was one person on a very low budget engaging in large international issues. I do not claim to have made a major impact. But I did manage to shake the tree and get my message across. When I was talking to Chinese officials in Beijing about the Dalai Lama, they asked me, "Why an American?" I told them that consultants are one of the largest exports from America. They never asked me why I was a private citizen and not a diplomat. They found that acceptable.

Governments may resist change, bend to change, or embrace change. But they are rarely the original source of change. The source of change is the greater soul of society; the flowering of aspirations deep in the souls of people that coalesce to form a collective and irresistible force. Underlying the flowering of human aspiration is, I think, an even deeper source of change: the spiritual force that feeds all of life. Government is even further removed from this.

If there are any pearls of wisdom I can extract from my experiences, they are twofold. First, to overcome the apparently insurmountable human problems facing the world, we must reconnect with our spiritual sources. Not necessarily through formal religious systems, but humanity must, in some way, look inward and explore spiritual solutions to old problems. Second, on a more practical level, governments must look more to the private sector for guidance and creative resources. To optimize our ability to overcome problems, governments and the private sector must make greater efforts to work in cooperation toward shared goals. These are not mind-shattering suggestions. But I think they get to the heart of the matter.

1

SPIRITUAL FOUNDATIONS

*Disciple: As I was watching the sun rise over the
mountains, the sunlight turned into
rivers of golden liquid light, flooding
the world and rushing through me. See
how the world sparkles!*

*Master: The world has not changed; you have
changed.*

Light and Compassion

MY DEEPEST MEMORIES of childhood are from moments of
silence. Walking down a trail in the hot pine-scented
woods of Georgia. Sitting in a school classroom with
wooden floors, high ceilings, and windows streaming with
light. Fishing in the early morning with my father and
watching the rising sun melt the mist away. Such experiences were permeated by a deep silence, where the sights,
smells, and feelings were extraordinarily vibrant and alive.
There was a presence around me, a grace. It was not me,
but something close to me and all about me. It was intan-
gible, but real. And I would lose myself in it.

In my teens, this presence slowly began to take the shape of a beautiful light. It was not a physical light. It did not cast shadows, and other people did not see it. It was, for lack of a better word, a spiritual light. The source of the light was not known to me. The light was just somehow there, and it had a soothing quality about it. It glittered about me and made the world sparkle. There was a magic about this light. It was as if its touch awakened the world about me. The sky and earth, the people, and common objects around me all began to take on an inner glow and vibrancy. Ever since this light emerged, I have not seen real darkness. When the sun goes down and the lights are turned off, this light always pulsates around me, like a natural night-light.

Everything I saw became intensely beautiful, that is, at least visually. I remember my many walks as a teen in the slums of Guatemala City, with its mud streets strewn with garbage and sewage and its children in rags. The light, glittering all about, gave the place a great beauty. It had a heavenly glow. But it was also ugly. It was beautiful and ugly at the same time. This experience has followed me throughout the years, in Washington, D.C.; New York City; India; China; Burma; and Afghanistan. Life is so divinely beautiful, yet we humans can make it so ugly. Or, as sometimes in my life I have thought, why is life so beautiful, and yet I am unhappy?

In my late teens, I began to become aware of the source of this light. It was a great sun. I had begun spending time in silent meditation, where I would sit with eyes closed and spine erect. A source of light would emerge, becoming brighter and brighter. My soul would touch this source of light, there would be an explosion of light, and then the source would recede into the background. Eventually, I could spend more time close to this sun. I would merge into it and spend one or two seconds in the vastness of brilliant light. The light was so bright that one or two seconds was all I could handle; then I'd be kicked out. If I had my own way, I would never leave.

The light was not like normal sunlight, where the brighter it is, the hotter and more harsh it feels. This light had the quality of consciousness, of being, of life. Most of all, it had the quality of joy. The closer I was to this inner sun, the brighter its light. But instead of the light blinding or burning, it simply gave more joy and bliss. It was the joy of the soul, not the senses. It was nirvana, the endless source of peace and life-energy for the soul. It was an ocean of peace for the river of a restless soul.

This spiritual sun soon settled into a permanent relationship with my soul. It now shines gently as a pool of white light over my chest. That is, it shines from there when I am awake with eyes open and gazing out in front me. Sometimes in silent moments I seem to almost gaze directly into it, but mostly it stays in the periphery of my vision. It is as if this sun does not want to get in the way when I am looking at something. With my eyes closed, it is just close by. Sometimes it is brighter than other times. But generally it is just here, reminding me of its presence. Over the years, I have slowly developed a closer relationship with this spiritual sun. It has become very much a part of me. But it has been a slow maturing process.

One of the great lessons of my youth was that I cannot force myself into the gates of heaven. My whole focus in life was to live permanently in the center of this newly discovered sun of my soul. But no amount of meditation or prayer was going to speed up a process that had its own natural time for development. My soul just did not have the capacity to withstand such intense light. It may take me lifetimes to develop the capacity to live in union with this sun. My soul had to be conditioned by labor and love, like the symbolic ancient Mason, who slowly built the temple of his soul block by block, until it was ready to house the Spirit of God; or like the Grail Knight, who must go through many trials before drinking from the Holy Grail.

Astronomers tell us that if we imagine the sun to be about three feet in diameter, then, proportionately, the Earth would be about the size of a green pea and would be orbiting about three hundred feet away, or about the distance of a football field, from the sun. Our souls, I like to think, are like little green peas orbiting at great distances from a spiritual sun. We orbit at the distance precisely right for us, not too far away to feel cold nor too close that we cannot stand the brilliance of the light. Over time, the orbit becomes closer, as we evolve to absorb more light, making our way to the brilliance of the center.

When I was still uncertain about what I was experiencing, I asked an old man who lectured on spirituality. He looked at me and said, "Oh, that's the light of the absolute, the highest light. It's the light of no shadows. You don't see any shadows do you? Very natural experience, very natural. The thing is to become the light, not simply to see it." It was all old hat to him, but very new to me.

I do not consider my spiritual sun to be God in the complete sense of the word, merely a portal into the vastness of the Spirit of God. The vastness of the physical cosmos (billions of galaxies) is, in a sense, the body of God. The spiritual aspect that underlies the universe must, of course, far exceed the body in depth and splendor. Imagine sitting on a beach by the Pacific Ocean with waves lapping over your legs. You would say that you are playing in the ocean. But in actuality, you are playing in a small part of it, with its vastness extending far out beyond your comprehension. The spiritual sun is the lapping of small waves from the unfathomable spiritual ocean of God. It is the soul's entrance into the infinite mystery of the Spirit.

Plato argued that the reason the soul can experience the divine is that the soul is made of the same stuff as the divine. The soul merging into Spirit is like water merging into water.

I could interpret my experiences through the eyes of many of the world's religious or spiritual doctrines. It may be the Holy Spirit, or Buddha's nirvana, or the transcendental Brahman of Lord Krishna. But this is merely academic. The important thing is the experience and its impact on the soul. I know it only as my spiritual source, my spiritual home and link to God. The world may come and go, but this spiritual sun is eternal. It is the eternity of the soul. I feel and know this intuitively.

The light I see in my soul shines in every soul. Most people do not see this light, but it is there. It is the life force that feeds the soul. Seeing it is just one way of experiencing it. It is not simply light, but pure Spirit. People sense it in many different ways: as a deep calm, as inspiration, as a presence, as tender love, as grace, as serenity, as beauty, as a bubbling of life from within, or as a majesty outside in the mountains and sky.

There are a number of "arguments" for the existence of God. The most common is the "argument by design." According to this argument, if there is a design, it follows that there must be a designer. If we find a watch washed up on the beach, we assume that it was created by someone and did not just somehow come together over millions of years. The more aware we become of the complexity and orderliness in the design of the universe—which far exceeds that of a watch—the more compelling the argument that there is a designer.

A modern variation of this argument is that if the forces that hold an atom together varied just the slightest, then there would be no hydrogen atom, and thus no sun, no sunshine, and no life. The narrow conditions in physics and biology in which life becomes possible imply that those conditions are purposeful and designed to be that way. However, my experience is that a person is never, or only rarely, convinced of the existence of a higher intelligence by an argument, no matter how compelling it may seem. It is their own direct intuition of a higher intelligence that convinces them. In moments of silence, looking up in the stars, watching a sunset or moonrise, or just during everyday experiences, a person may come to sense a profound beauty and intelligence. It is this deep sense of beauty in life that awakens an intuitive certainty that there is a higher intelligence.

My gift, if I have one, is a gift of experiencing spiritual energy as an inner light. My eyes have been turned a hundred and eighty degrees so that I can see the spiritual energy that connects my soul to the eternal Spirit. This is not an uncommon experience, at least among the chronicles of spiritual experiences. Nor is it any more profound than the intuitive feeling of a spiritual presence. But it does have the advantage of making spirituality as real to me as is my hand in front of my face. It is a constant reminder of my destiny as a soul, and it tends to keep me out of trouble. That is, at least spiritually. I still get into trouble in the world.

I LIVED IN Guatemala for a couple of years when I was a teenager. Like most Latin American countries, Guatemala is very poor, with its wealth concentrated in a small upper class. The majority of the people are descendants from the Mayan Indians, who populate the bottom of the social ladder. And yet it is the Mayan Indians that give Guatemala its color and cultural beauty.

As adolescents, my friends and I would roam the streets and countryside like little spoiled kings, viewing the world as our own. During one of these roamings, feeling tired, I laid on the side of the road to rest and gaze at the sky. My mind became expanded as if extended across the land. I felt the presence of a people stretching from a distant time to the present, crying out under great oppression. I felt the deep sorrow of a people who have been trampled on, hurt, and neglected. Such a deep, deep sorrow. It crushed me. This vision remained in my mind all that day, like the lingering smell of incense.

After this vision, I had a deeper awareness of what these people have gone through. I was not oblivious to it before. But for a fleeting moment, I was no longer a casual onlooker from the outside. I was participating in the inner side of their life, in their soulful longing. It was the difference between wearing gloves to feel an object and feeling an object with naked hands. It is much more real, and it made me a more serious adolescent.

Some years after, while in meditation, the earth appeared to me as if I were looking down from space. It was alive, translucent blue, and radiant, spinning slowly in space. Suddenly, blood appeared around the living planet, and my heart was struck as I felt its life. Again, I became aware of a sorrow and pain emerging from the distant past and crying out in the present. Images floated past of faces choked with tears and anguish; hands in prayer surrounded by burning flames begging for an answer, but getting none; heads hung down in hopelessness and defeat. It was not the images that were crushing. These I can get from the local video store. It was the life crying out; it was the spirit pushing forth from these images and permeating me. I became that sorrow. I was lost in it. It was so overwhelming that I felt at the brink of death.

As if in response, waves of compassion flowed through me, and I felt the peace of the stillness after a thunderstorm. I left my body and looked down on myself as a stranger. My body began to be filled with golden light and turned into a body of gold. A voice said, "This is the body of Christ." The vision ended and I returned to my body.

Trying to make sense of visions is not easy. They are, I think, very personal. But the most important aspect of a vision is not a hidden message but its impact on the soul. These were maturing experiences, like the changing voice in a growing boy or the sprouting seed responding to the warmth of sunlight. These visions shattered the wall of my mind and released a force that was pushing forth. I saw that I am not separate from the world but connected to it by Spirit.

For many, this realization seeps in slowly through a maturing process. Perhaps I was so dense that I needed a ton of bricks on my head to make a strong impact. These visions marked my passage to manhood.

The sword thrust into my heart by these visions brought forth the waters of compassion. This is, I think, the real meaning of the words "body of Christ." My body was beginning to house compassion, the essence of the teaching of Christ. The Lord's Prayer is a prayer of forgiveness: asking forgiveness from God and pledging forgiveness to others. Forgiveness opens the heart and allows the healing powers of compassion to flow into the world.

The phenomenon of Christ was not merely a doctrine. The real phenomenon of Christ was a spiritual force that he put forth into the world to stir the latent seeds of compassion in humanity. When Christ was on the cross, he sent such a tidal wave of compassion into the world that one can still feel it today.

Compassion and its mother, love, are the great elixirs of life—the healing waters for humanity. The light of pure Spirit gives sustenance and peace to the soul and leads it to its spiritual destiny. These are the essentials for a world that longs to heal itself and find peace.

Law and Policy

AFTER COLLEGE, I spent some time as a sculptor. But I could not stay in my studio. I always wanted to get out and do something. What exactly, I did not know. So, during a trip to India in 1986, I decided to go to either law school or graduate school in philosophy when I returned to the United States. This was a crossroads decision. One path would lead me into the practical world, the other into the academic world. I chose the practical path and still wonder whether it was the better choice, or whether it was "practical."

The study of law is much like the study of philosophy. The study of philosophy teaches the student about the reasoning process. The student does not study only, for example, what Plato said or what Hume said, but primarily the reasoning that led to their conclusions. Law school attempts a similar thing: to teach people how to think for themselves. It also teaches the student how to research and argue the law. After three years of law school, a student may not know any more about common-day law, such as municipal or criminal codes, than before law school, but that student can research, reason, and argue the law.

In the American common-law system, the law is not a series of easily accessible rules. The law is embedded in the opinions of judges found in myriad court cases. The opinions of judges must be consulted even for the interpretation of written statutes and regulations. The law is also in constant flux by actions in the courts or the legislature.

Most of the time in law school is spent reading opinions. In a typical opinion, the judge reviews the competing arguments in the case, then develops his own argument, which forms the basis of his conclusion, called the "holding" of the case. The law is constantly being reconstructed from the ground up in these cases. Classes are spent arguing whether the judge's reasoning was correct. In the future, some of these students will be involved in changing the law, either through courts or the legislature.

The law is thus reasoned. Lawyers are professional arguers, which is why they can sometimes be a headache to talk to. Thomas Jefferson once remarked that he would never concede any point to his chief justice, John Marshall, because Marshall would then use it as a premise to elegantly build an airtight argument: "If you concede this, then you must concede this because . . ." and so forth. Many lawyers degenerate the reasoning process to the point of sophistry. Here the object is winning a case, often by deception and obfuscation, without any regard to exploring justice. But legal trickery can only take one so far. In the end, the law must have rational integrity or it collapses.

The perfect law, I think, is the law of love. The story of Lucifer, Prince of Mind, is the story of an archangel that attempted to exalt reason over love. As a result, he was thrown down. Nothing is above love, the story proclaims. Love underlies reason, balances it, and gives it life and purpose. This subject is rarely touched on in law school except in philosophical discussions on justice, equity, and public policy. Ideally, the written law is tempered with the judge's own sense of justice and compassion. The wise judge remains an ideal in our tumultuous world.

Much is written about law school. But in the end, it is just school. You go to class, argue with teachers, take exams, and when bored, fall asleep. Most law schools have ranking systems. So in a class of a hundred and ten people you will fall somewhere between one and a hundred and ten, depending on your grades. Because the people on the top have the best shot at the highest-paying jobs, the system encourages competition and an adversarial attitude among the students. Some students are dragged into this vortex of insanity. But most, including myself, considered the system an anachronism to be tolerated.

To some extent, this is a reflection of the American adversarial system of law. The idea is that lawyers are adversaries locked in battle. Truth is supposed to emerge from this battle. This makes for good drama on TV, but it is not always effective. When Mahatma Gandhi began practicing law, he discovered that two things happen when a case goes to court: parties remain enemies for life, and it is very costly. By mediating a dispute outside of court, the parties can be reconciled as friends, and it is not as costly. The highest destiny of a lawyer, Gandhi reasoned, is to mediate, not litigate. Thus, even in the American adversarial system, most disputes between private citizens are resolved outside of courts.

By nature, I am more inclined to be a mediator than a litigator. I did not take any courses in trial law. My favorite courses were jurisprudence, international law, human rights law, constitutional law, and comparative law (Hindu law, Islamic law, Chinese law, European law).

After law school, I went to Washington, D.C., and enrolled in a LLM program in international and comparative law at George Washington University. In law, the degrees are backwards: the first degree is the Juris Doctor (JD); and the second is the Master of Laws (LLM). The whole process took a number of years.

While in Washington, D.C., I worked in the U.S. State Department's legal division. "L," as it is called, attempts to give "impartial" advice to the State Department and White House on international legal matters; it also helps to justify U.S. decisions that fall in the gray areas of international law, such as the U.S. decision to mine Nicaragua's waters or to engage in war against Panama. International law is an evolving body of law, and the United States has considerable influence in the direction it is evolving. "L" is always in the middle of this. This influence is usually good, such as the push for democracy as a basic human right. But sometimes it is questionable.

I was at "L" in the aftermath of the Gulf War and during the Bosnia crisis. I was a peon, not involved in the big issues. Mostly, I processed claims by U.S. citizens against Iraq for loss of property or personal injuries resulting from Iraq's invasion of Kuwait. Money to compensate these people is supposed to come from the sale of Iraqi oil. The only case I remember working on was that of a U.S. Marine pilot shot down during the war. When he was captured, he was beaten up, taken to an army post and beaten up again, and then given to civilian onlookers, who beat him up. Then they took him to a jail, where he was beaten on a regular basis. He remembered the first couple of days. The rest was a blur.

Under the program, he was to be given compensation for mental distress and physical injuries. What I found disturbing was that compensation for human loss and injury was limited, whereas compensation for property loss was not. More would be given for a lost house than for a lost child. But this was all in theory. It was a failed program.

Saddam Hussein was not interested in compensating people, and has refused to sell oil for this purpose. The subsequent economic sanctions that were put in place to force Saddam to comply with this and other measures have only managed to hurt the poor and the weak. This means mostly children, who have died of lack of proper medicine and nutrition, thus compounding the tragedy. The better policy would have been for the allied forces to have taken Saddam out during the war. This is a good example where mediation and economic sanctions have failed.

SOME PEOPLE DECLARE that the United States should not be the world's policeman. But I have never had a problem with this, at least with the United States, being in a leadership role in forming coalitions among nations to deal with serious world problems. George Washington warned that the United States should not get entangled in foreign disputes, and this warning dominated U.S. foreign policy for the first hundred years or so after he said it. It made good sense, because the United States was in its infancy and needed to concentrate on its own development. But U.S. policy was forced to change after World War I, when the mantle of world power shifted from Great Britain to the United States. With power comes responsibility, and with world power comes global responsibility. The United States did not really have a choice in the matter; the responsibility fell into its lap.

Great Britain presided as the world power during the zenith of the era of sea power, when the international community became united by the seas through commerce and, sadly, through the violent colonization of the world by European powers. But one thing Great Britain accomplished as a world power was the eradication of the slave trade on the high seas. They did this on their own initiative by a unilateral police action against slave ships. This is a point many have forgotten.

When the mantle of world power shifted to the United States, the world was entering into what some call the era of air. Air travel was in its infancy and became instrumental, along with telecommunications, in hastening world integration. America's role seems to be in resisting tyranny in its many forms so that the world may integrate, not by force, but freely through common interests. Or to put it in a more spiritual light, the U.S. role is to ensure that the world is united by the bonds of love instead of oppression.

Ultimately, only love can unite. Forced unity always fails. Like the Soviet Union and Yugoslavia, forced unity eventually degenerates and implodes or explodes. Alexander the Great, Gaius Julius Caesar, Charlemagne, and Napoleon Bonaparte attempted to cloak aggression with nobility of purpose. Alexander, for example, began his mornings with prayers; he conquered peoples under a royal banner of the Great King and did his best to befriend those he conquered. But in the end, such efforts remained a cloak, their fruits limited and tainted with blood.

Admittedly, U.S. foreign policy is all-too-human, but its underlying purpose remains just. The United States resisted tyranny in the two world wars and the Cold War. At the end of World War II, America lifted the vanquished Germany back on its feet through the Marshall Plan. The same was done with Japan, where American lawyers helped to draft a new constitution, unamended to this day, that defined a new democratic Japan. The Japanese people, expecting American "demons," met smiling soldiers offering chocolate bars. This policy of compassion was uncommon in world history, where victors often acted with vengeance and oppression toward the vanquished. Compassion and the encouragement of democratic reform prevented the seeds of tyranny from being planted and thus sprouting in future generations. The oppressive measures against Germany after World War I, helped fuel the passions for World War II.

During the Cold War, the Soviet Union supported revolutions throughout the world, in Latin America, Africa, and Asia. The Soviet Union would take advantage of discontented people living under oppressive governments, providing them with the arms and Marxist ideology for revolution. The United States would counter the Soviets by supporting governments resisting Marxist revolutions. This often put the United States in the awkward position of supporting military regimes and dictators, which the United States is supposed to oppose.

America compensated by trying to push some of these oppressive governments toward democracy. This put much of the Third World between a rock (Soviet Union) and a hard place (the United States), turning the world into a battlefield between two superpowers that were fighting mainly through proxy armies in civil wars. One result was that this pressure forced many countries like El Salvador and Guatemala toward more democratic practices to avoid destruction by civil war. It was a very bloody, costly, and inefficient process that left much of the Third World deeply scarred. Years after leaving "L," I came face to face with this bitter fruit of the Cold War in the war-torn fields of Afghanistan.

Marxism arose in reaction to economic exploitation by nineteenth-century capitalism (the kind so well portrayed by Charles Dickens). Marxism envisioned the working class revolting and then ruling over an egalitarian society. Communism arose to champion this cause. But twentieth-century communism devolved to be a much greater source of exploitation and tyranny than nineteenth-century capitalism. Democracy proved the true champion of the Marxist cause through labor unions, labor laws, and general economic and social development. Interestingly, Mikhail Gorbachev, the last steward of the Soviet Union, argues that true socialism (where, according to him, every person is ensured a dignified level of existence, socially, economically and ecologically) can only be built through a democracy.

The end of the Cold War opened a new arena, and U.S. policymakers were uncertain as to what the U.S. role should be. I was at "L" during the Bosnia affair. The United States had hesitated for a couple of years while atrocities were being committed. State Department officials were resigning in disgust and protest. Eventually, the United States began a bombing campaign that quickly forced a peace agreement that ended the atrocities. What had been happening was that the United States deferred policy matters to the Europeans, who could not make the hard decisions. Secretary of State Warren Christopher later remarked that he and the administration did not realize how critically important U.S. leadership was; that it was a great mistake not to have taken the lead earlier.

Later came the genocide in Rwanda. The United States and the United Nations stood by and did nothing. It was not as if they were caught by surprise. Good intelligence was available indicating that a genocide was brewing. It is not clear to me what action would have been best to have prevented the genocide. But it is clear that something should have been done. The United States should have taken a leadership role in countering a looming genocide.

Then there was Kosovo. People may argue whether greater diplomatic skill and economic sanctions should have been used instead of military force. They also may argue if military force should have begun earlier and with the use of ground troops to prevent Serbian aggression against the people of Kosovo. But the underlying cause was just. With U.S. leadership, NATO made a strong statement to the world: mass murder and ethnic cleansing are not acceptable. True, NATO is a European defense organization, and its reach does not extend to other regions such as Rwanda. But, because NATO is composed of leading democratic nations, the message does have a global ring to it. It is the ring of destiny.

As the case of Kosovo reveals, policing is not an easy job. It is, after all, a response to the most gruesome and atrocious of human events. Nor does it address the more fundamental issue of the underlying cause of conflict and the source of real peace. The great challenge is to support those forces in the world that give rise to peace so that policing is not necessary.

President Woodrow Wilson declared that the United States should work to make the world safe for democracy. President Franklin Roosevelt resolved that the United States should endeavor to establish a "moral order" in the world by promoting the "four freedoms": freedom of speech, freedom of religion, freedom from want, and freedom from fear. "Freedom," he said, meant the "supremacy of human rights everywhere." The promotion of democracy and human rights represents the high ideals of U.S. foreign policy; it is the stuff of *moralpolitik,* which puts morals at center stage, versus *realpolitik,* which concentrates on power relations among competing nations. This aspect of U.S. foreign policy represents America's highest and best destiny.

Both Immanuel Kant, in his little book, *Perpetual Peace*, and Thomas Paine, in his classic work, *The Rights of Man*, argued that world peace becomes possible once all nations become democracies. History supports this theory: democracies tend not to go to war with other democracies. The United States may bomb a Saddam or a Milosevic, but never Canada or the United Kingdom.

Kant and Paine reasoned that popular opinion is always opposed to war, and thus democracies, being sensitive to popular opinion, will not fight each other. Paine further reasoned that because democracies are sensitive to the needs of the people, democracy provides the foundation for human rights, thus making it the key to both world peace and domestic peace within nations.

The UN Charter and the Universal Declaration of Human Rights both place the protection of human rights as the foundation of world peace. The implication is that it is the accumulated effect of vast numbers of exploited and victimized individuals that erupts into civil wars within nations and international wars between nations.

Human rights constitutes a vast body of international law, with the Universal Declaration at its core. It includes not only the civil rights that we are familiar with, such as equality before the law, freedom of expression, and freedom from arbitrary arrest, but also political rights, such as the right to free and fair elections; and the duty of governments to protect the environment and to address the economic, health, and educational needs of their people. The universality of human rights implies a spiritual unity of the human race. Traditions and values may vary, but they all orbit around core values present in the depths of the human soul.

Our understanding of democracy is refined through the lenses of human rights. Democracy is not simply governments that have elections, but governments that are also sensitive to the needs of their populace in specific ways. It is human rights standards that measure the worth and legitimacy of governments. A country like Mexico may be called a "democracy" because it holds elections, but it does not represent what most of us consider as democracy because of its widespread human rights abuses. Such a country is therefore sometimes called an "emerging" democracy. But, of course, an "emerging" democracy and "developed" are relative concepts. The United States is still struggling with its own democracy.

Conventional wisdom thus holds that democracy and human rights form the foundations for peace. More precisely, the foundations for peace are the higher thinking and spiritual forces stirring within humans that create democracy and human rights. The underlying spiritual forces are what is fundamental. The great war is fought in the souls of humans, and ultimately it is there that peace is found. These spiritual forces—the "milk" of human kindness, the "gentle rain" of human compassion, the soothing light of wisdom—are the unseen foundations of peace. These unseen spiritual forces spring forth from the human spirit and crystallize into the great complexities of democratic and human rights-based institutions.

The United States is seen as the model in the world for democracy and human rights, yet America is not at peace with itself. Violence flourishes in its streets, schools, and homes. For complete peace to dawn, compassion must soak into every fiber of human society.

If we categorize the levels of human conflict, we find that international wars are the easiest to resolve. Civil wars are much more difficult to resolve, and civil strife such as street violence is the most difficult to resolve. Since World War II, there have not been many international conflicts, and the world does not seem far away from international peace. Most recent wars have been civil wars. More prevalent are the violent crimes and civil unrest within nations. Humans are inherently resistant to change, so change tends to be slow and painful. But the unfolding of peace on its many levels, although slow to come, may be as inevitable as the coming of spring. Inevitable, because humanity is pregnant with this ideal.

WHEN I LEFT "L," I picked up an official copy of the Great Seal of the United States for my boss, the legal adviser, and my coworkers to sign. The Great Seal can be seen on the one dollar bill. The front of the seal is the bald eagle, which is also used as the U.S. coat of arms. The reverse side is often referred to as the "spiritual" side: the all-seeing eye of God on top of a pyramid, radiating a spiritual light, called the "blaze of glory." It is this symbol that I identified with. The eagle also has spiritual significance, for it flies above the clouds of discord and comes to us as a messenger from on high. But the eye of God is so very clear; anyone can see that there is a spiritual message.

Benjamin Franklin, Thomas Jefferson, and James Madison composed the original committee that recommended the all-seeing eye as the central symbol of the Great Seal. When the Great Seal was placed on the dollar bill, the all-seeing eye was put on the right side of the bill. This was because we read from left to right, making the right side the less prominent position, and thus more suitable for the reverse side of the seal. President Franklin Roosevelt initially approved the placement, but then changed his mind, reversing the placement so that the all-seeing eye was on the left, making the subtle point that spirituality should be primary in American life.

There is a famous picture of George Washington kneeling in prayer in the snow at Valley Forge. There is a less famous story of a vision that Washington had at Valley Forge during his darkest moments when the prospects seemed dim that his ragtag and ill-equipped group of men could ever overcome the greatest empire the world had ever seen. Washington was sitting in his office when a woman appeared. At first he thought it was a real woman and began to address her. Then he suddenly found himself unable to speak. The woman said, "Son of the Republic, look and learn," and a vision unfolded to Washington in which he saw the colonists overcoming the British through the aid of a great angel.

Whether or not the story is accurate, it portrays the belief of Washington and other founding fathers that they were guided by a higher power, that the United States was formed in accord with a grand design. In the writings of Washington, you can sense more than a belief. In fact, you can sense a genuine feeling of intimacy with something higher. Thus the all-seeing eye is often called the Eye of Providence. Above the eye are the Latin words *annuit coeptis*, meaning He (God) has favored our undertakings. Under the eye are the Latin words *novus ordo seclorum*, meaning a new order has begun.

The old order gripping the world at that time was feudalism, in which sovereignty was vested in kings and aristocracies. The new order is democracy, in which sovereignty is vested in the people, and government acts in their trust. America represented the first sprouting of a new order that is just now beginning to sweep the world. The emergence of American democracy was a critical point in world history. America's beginning was tainted by slavery, oppression of native Americans, and general economic exploitation, the effects of which America is still overcoming. But this is to be expected. There is no other place for a new order to begin than in the womb of an old order.

Many of the founding fathers were members of the Masons, a fraternity dedicated to the building of the soul. The pyramid under the all-seeing eye symbolizes the soul that we are all in the process of building. In the case of the Great Seal, it is the soul of the nation. The meaning here is that the eye of God guides our souls and the nation. But it also implies that without this guidance, the nation will flounder and collapse. It is a constant reminder of the source of our wisdom.

I was at "L" on a nine-month contract. Just a month before I left, I got a letter from the Dalai Lama's Constitution Redrafting Committee asking me if I would advise them in the drafting of a constitution for Tibet. The Dalai Lama, of course, was in exile from Tibet. But he hoped to return. The constitution was to be a model for a democratic government in Tibet that he would establish upon his return.

A year earlier I had done volunteer work for a Tibetan organization that included writing guidelines for drafting a constitution, and that work had impressed the chairman of the Constitution Redrafting Committee, Juchen Thupten Namgyal. This was just the sort of thing that I went to school for, so I was excited even though there was no salary, just "expenses paid." I am essentially a creative entity and too independent for work in an institution like the State Department. Nine months was just enough time to get some appreciation of how things work in a government agency. It was time for me to go forth and test my skills as a peacemaker, as a promoter of democracy and human rights in the battlefield of life.

2

TIBET

Disciple: What is the essence of an adviser?

*Master: Sometimes it is to be a healer by words
and presence. Sometimes it is to be an
irritating voice that people wish to
silence. But always it is to step aside
and let a higher voice reveal itself.*

Dharmsala

THE TIBETAN CULTURE has thrived for centuries on the
"roof of the world," a high plateau in the Himalayan
Mountains. The remoteness of the Himalayas allowed for
the evolution of a unique culture centered around Tibetan
Buddhism. The Dalai Lama was both head of religion and
head of government. In 1951 China annexed Tibet by
force. After years of trying to work with the Chinese, the
Dalai Lama fled Tibet for exile in India in 1959. Ever

since then, the Dalai Lama has been trying to work things out with China to preserve the Tibetan culture and allow for his return to Tibet.

My mission took me back to India. I arrived in New Delhi seven years after the end of my first trip there. This time I was greeted at the airport by a smiling Tibetan girl, who was waving a sign with my name on it. India is a world unto itself, a colorful mix of many religions, cultures, and languages. It is a land where the highest and the lowest, the most spiritual and most worldly, and everything in between, bustles about in a great circus of life. India has a feeling about it, an atmosphere that like a fragrance or taste, is real but difficult to describe.

From New Delhi, I took a sleeper train to Pathunkat, near Dharmsala, where I was met by the general secretary of the Constitution Redrafting Committee. The secretary was looking for a tall fat man with gray hair, his idea of an American legal adviser who had worked at the State Department. I was an unshaven short, slim man with dark hair and wearing blue jeans, so it took some time for us to connect.

Dharmsala is at the foothills of the Himalayas. About a half-hour walk up into the foothills is the Dalai Lama's administration; another twenty minutes above that is the Dalai Lama's home and office; and five minutes from that is a little village called McLeod Ganj, where most Tibetans in the area live. This whole area is spotted throughout with Buddhist monasteries and temples.

The McLeod culture is a playful mix of Tibetans and Western tourists who come there for Buddhist studies or just to hang out in an exciting place. I would often have my dinners in McLeod Ganj, which included a brisk twenty-minute hike uphill from the administration area where I lived. There were no street lights, and at times it would be so dark I could not see the road. All I could see would be waves of light all about me, pulsating from my spiritual sun, so I would feel my way with my feet, occasionally stumbling from the many holes in the road.

FOR MUCH OF the time I lived in Dharmsala, I stayed in an apartment overlooking a monastery. Every morning at about 4:30 the monks rang prayer bells. The sound was so loud that it would fill the valley, and I was just fifty feet away. It was annoying at first, but then I got accustomed to the sound and eventually became fond of it. The crisp ring would wake me sharply from my sleep, and my mind would float on the sounds of the bells as if they were ocean waves, or air currents. After the last bell sounded, the sound would linger in the mountain air, gently leading me back to sleep.

My bed was next to a large picture window facing the east and overlooking the monastery, a valley below, and distant foothills. So I would wake up again at the first rays of dawn. I would sit up and meditate on my inner sun, occasionally opening my eyes to watch the progression of the physical sun as it rose over the horizon, stretching its beauty over the earth. Then I would lie back down and go into the sweetest of sleeps. These were good mornings.

Besides serving the obvious purpose of an alarm clock, the bells are meant to raise the vibrations of the monastery, preparing it for the morning practice of meditation, prayers, and *pujas* (ceremonies). It is often said that everything is a vibration of energy. Whether it be the most gross matter or the most refined spiritual thought, it is all vibrations of various forms of energy. Spiritual development is sometimes characterized as a process of raising our vibrations to resonate with the higher vibrations of the divine.

The bells were so penetrating that they seemed to go into your bones, making the whole body and even the buildings resonate with its rings. After the monastery becomes alive and vibrant with the sounding of bells, the monks begin the more subtle spiritual practice of reciting scriptures, prayers, and mantras, all aimed at bringing the soul to the highest spiritual vibration they are capable of.

Bringing the vibrations up is one thing, but maintaining them at a high level becomes a life-long endeavor. This is a common experience in everyday life. In moments of inspiration, we may make resolutions to change, for example to stop getting angry or stop smoking. But when the inspiration is gone, it is difficult to follow through on the resolution. It is even more difficult to sustain when the inspiration is ignited from outside and not self-generated.

Gregorian chants in the Western monastic tradition have a similar effect of "putting wings on the soul," lifting the spirit up to feel a sense of holiness. I have some aunts who, whenever they get together, belt out gospel songs, which transport them for the moment to another place. It seems to be a major part of their spiritual path.

On a more mundane level is the endless stream of music on the airwaves that keeps people bopping about with the tunes and the many feelings invoked. Music is a universal language. Rock and roll, specifically the Beatles, was perhaps the first global cultural event. It united much of the world's youth through a common form of vibration.

A major part of rock and roll invoked feelings of forceful transformation, a "let's break the boundaries" type of feeling. The Beatles's music was by far the most influential at the time, but was primarily about love. Much of this was romantic love, such as in "Julia," but some of it went to a higher spiritual note, as in "All You Need Is Love," "Let it Be," and "The Long and Winding Road." John Lennon's "Give Peace a Chance" became a global mantra for peace.

When today's generation listen to the Beatles, they may find it hard to understand why that band had such a wide appeal. It was, as Lennon later remarked, a cultural phenomenon; it struck a common chord in the people at that time. It is impossible to measure the impact of their music in influencing the thinking of the youth. But clearly there was some type of spiritual impact.

Some believe that the earth as a whole is slowly raising its vibrations. The idea is that spiritual evolution is a global event and humans are a part of the process, but not all of the process. The earth, having an organic quality, has a way of self-healing and purification and may directly affect human evolution, as human life affects the life of Earth. Perhaps the most critical point in human spiritual evolution is the transition between the life of violence and the life of peace. I believe we are reaching that point. The twentieth century has been the most violent century in human history; perhaps the twenty-first century may prove to be the most peaceful century. Of course, outer peace is a reflection of inner peace. To achieve that peace, humanity must return to the wisdom of the Buddha and other spiritual "lighthouses."

THE STORY OF Lord Buddha is a story of an Indian crown prince who rejected the life of royalty to pursue enlightenment. After years of struggle, Buddha attained enlightenment and began a teaching centered around nirvana: freedom in the ocean of divine consciousness. Buddha was a religious reformer who restored the path to enlightenment in a society that was lost on the superficial level of ceremony and ritual. Whereas Krishna and Christ are considered to be God coming down to Earth, Buddha is considered to be a man who rose to God. The impact Buddha had on the world is some indication of the depth of his teachings and spiritual attainment.

Tibetan Buddhism incorporates tantra and shamanism, making it one of the most colorful branches of Buddhism. Tantra is a body of practices for spiritual development involving, among other things, the use of mantras and visualization of deities during meditation. Tibetan monasteries and homes are full of *tankas* (religious paintings), which depict the great complexity of Tibetan deities and mythologies. This elevates the painter to a high position in Tibetan society. The vast array of deities in the Tibetan pantheon is confusing until you consider them, like the Hindu gods, to represent different aspects of one underlying divinity, represented by Lord Buddha. This complexity of practices and beliefs directs the Buddhist to the singularity of divine consciousness.

Shamanism is often associated with the spirit world. A common practice is mediumship, where a spirit enters the body of a person (the medium) to use it as an instrument for communication. Personally, I would never give my body over to another spirit, unless it was an archangel, who, I am sure, would find little use for my small restrictive body. But that's just me.

In Tibetan Buddhism, the practice of mediumship is used by oracles, who consider the spirits to be deities. The Dalai

Lama and his administration have a few "state" oracles, who answer questions dealing only with political matters. Tibetan officials have mixed feelings about the oracles. As depicted in the movie *Kundun*, the oracle did rightly advise the Dalai Lama to leave Tibet before it was too late; but apparently the oracles are not always right or sometimes are too vague. The problem with vagueness is illustrated by the Greek story of the king who went to the ancient oracle of Delphi. The oracle told him that he would be the cause of the downfall of a great nation. Excited by the prospect, he made war against a great nation. He lost the war, causing the downfall of his own great nation.

I went to a private Tibetan oracle called Yutima. The oracle, an older woman, was dressed in colorful robes and wore a crown and a brass breastplate that "mirrored" the deity. After the burning of earthy incense and recitation of Buddhist sutras, she entered a trance. With eyes closed, she began chanting in an old formal Tibetan tongue and told me I had a beautiful girlfriend in America (true) and would help improve human rights in Tibet (I tried).

Over the years I have seen a few oracles, astrologers, clairvoyants and, in Dharmsala, Tibetan Lamas doing *"mo"* with the use of dice, or *malas*, reading them like Tarot cards or tea leaves in a cup. Sometimes they were accurate about my life; sometimes wrong. If taken lightly, I think they can be useful as a way of reflecting on one's life. But taken too seriously, they can be dangerous. Even if a clairvoyant is right about your life, this person's advice can still be as bad as that of the local bartender. In my experience, being clairvoyant does not always translate into being wise.

I met an old pundit in New Delhi who could read a person's mind. He would ask, "How many questions do you have?" The person would tell him the number. Then the pundit would write the questions down and hand it to the person, beaming with joy at his ability. This gift gave people confidence in his abilities. The trouble was that although he was always right about what the questions were, his advice was not very good.

With oracles, as with any advice that comes our way, our own silent inner voice is the final authority. As the saying goes, a king should listen to counsel, but in the end he should be his own counsel. It always goes back to the silent knowing of one's self. Without that as a point of reference, we are lost. In this respect, oracles are best used, if at all, in stimulating that inner voice. All of life can be seen as an oracle: people, mountains and streams, comics—anything that jars and awakens our awareness.

BASIC TO BUDDHISM is the doctrine of reincarnation. It is a compelling belief and simple in concept: the soul, being immortal, evolves through time from spiritual infancy to spiritual perfection through a cycle of birth, death, and rebirth. After a lifetime of experiences, the body dies and the soul returns to its spiritual home. The metaphorical "gatekeeper of heaven" is unimpressed by narrow human values, such as career accomplishments, and accepts as "payment" only the virtue and spirituality the soul has gained. Infused with a higher divine wisdom, the eyes of the soul are open, and it feels the sharp pangs of its mistakes and warm joys of its successes in life. In this way, the experiences of its life are incorporated into the soul as wisdom.

The wiser soul, having rested in its spiritual womb, is born again. Usually it forgets its previous births but takes with it the wisdom it has gained from those births to pursue a new life with new challenges. Thus the wheel of birth and death goes on. "Practice makes perfect," and so the constant practice of living through innumerable lives eventually creates a perfected soul. For Buddhists, Buddha's nirvana is the fulfillment of this cycle and thus the end to human suffering.

The doctrine, of course, is prevalent throughout the world and extends far beyond the Buddhists and Hindus. At the end of *The Republic*, Plato recounts the vision of Er, a soldier who dies in battle and goes to heaven. In heaven he watches the cycle of birth, death, and rebirth.

When the hero Odysseus was given a choice of a new life, he remembered his former hardships and thus sought a life of a private man with no cares. New lifetimes were written on tablets and given on a first-come, first-served basis, and this particular tablet of a simple man was hard to find because it had been lying about on the ground neglected by everyone else. Before the souls were reborn, they drank from the River of Forgetfulness, but the drink was withheld from Er, who was sent back to his body on the battlefield to tell his story.

One of the defining characteristics of Tibetan Buddhism is that the great lamas (spiritual teachers) are considered to be reincarnations of previous great lamas. Today's Dalai Lama is said to be his fourteenth incarnation as the Dalai Lama, thus his title, "the Fourteenth Dalai Lama." The discovery of the incarnation of the Panchen Lama reveals the complexity of the process. A search committee was formed in Tibet to find the child. Following dreams and omens, the committee decided on a few candidates for the incarnation. This was shared with the Dalai Lama who, because of the importance of the incarnation, selected the child from among the candidates by using his own oracle process.

When he announced the selection in 1995, the Chinese became furious. The Panchen Lama, like the Dalai Lama, has a political as well as a religious role in Tibet. In fact, the Panchen Lama is considered to be the second most powerful political leader in Tibet next to the Dalai Lama. So the Chinese considered the selection to be a political act. Because the Chinese were in political conflict with the Dalai Lama, they rejected his selection and had one of the other candidates selected.

The result is that there are now two Panchen Lamas in Tibet. One child has the backing of the Chinese. The other child, rejected and isolated by the Chinese, is now believed to be held with his family in Beijing under house arrest. I remember that a few years earlier, when the previous Panchen Lama died, the Chinese declared that he could only reincarnate inside China (including Tibet). It struck me as funny because the Chinese were, in a sense, asserting jurisdiction over heaven.

The Dalai Lama does not claim to remember his past incarnations, but he does claim to feel a special connection to the previous Dalai Lamas. I have always had doubts as to whether today's lamas are indeed reincarnations of specific lamas of earlier days. However, there appears to be an ability to find children that have the spiritual development needed to fulfill the responsibilities of a lama. I do not think it is flawless, but there is a tendency for it to work. This is the important thing.

According to the doctrine of reincarnation, if a child is highly spiritual, it is because the child has attained that in the past. Thus, recognizing a child to be the reincarnation of a specific lama may be historically inaccurate, but it would be true to the general theory of reincarnation if the child is spiritually developed. Other cultures, like the American Indians, have their own traditions on how to recognize a child that has the "right stuff" to be a spiritual teacher. The value of this is that it provides spiritual training at a young age.

I do not remember past lives, though I have met people who claim they do. A lecturer I have heard on many occasions tells the story of being instructed in the "school of mysteries." When the lesson of reincarnation came up, he was given the experience of a previous lifetime. All of a sudden he was an Egyptian, standing under a hot sun and sweating. The memory was so clear it was as if he were reliving it. He was there for a few moments and then back again. Experience is the best teacher.

People often tell me that I have had distant lifetimes as a soldier and more recently as a monk. This makes sense. These two qualities are amusingly revealed in an experience I had as a child sitting on a railing at an Air Force yacht club as my father was talking to his fighter-pilot buddies. As I listened, I went into a deep meditation, became unconscious of my surroundings, and fell over backwards into the water below. The military past brought me into military surroundings, and my monkish past made me prone to meditation.

I have always felt comfortable around the military. And in my teens and twenties, meditations often had images of violence and gore, welling up from the deep past. But there is no attachment to the military. The passion, whatever it was, has long gone. The monk part is much stronger in my life. Images of Christ and other religious figures have always filled my meditations. I feel very comfortable around monks and monasteries, go through long periods of celibacy, and often spend time as a recluse. But I am no longer a monk. That is also gone, except for the spiritual inclination.

The consequences of past lifetimes are present in the circumstances of our lives and the thoughts and images flowing through our souls. This is our karma, as the Buddhists and Hindus say. It creates the environment for us to evolve; it is our curse and our blessing.

KARMA LITERALLY MEANS "action," but the word is used to refer to the broader doctrine dealing with the consequences of human actions in a moral universe. The basic principle of karma is that we are responsible for what we set in motion. Karma maintains balance in life and keeps us going on an evolutionary path. Ancient cultures envisioned gods throwing down evils and miseries to punish us, or showering fortunes to reward us. But if we consider karma to be the operation of a higher intelligence, then it would be a mistake to project the lower human motives of revenge, anger, or pride to this doctrine. Karma is more properly a higher love and wisdom that maintains the moral balance in the universe. Being thus, karma is something I cannot pretend to fathom. I can only struggle with simple notions of responsibility and evolution.

If we send an iota of hate into the world, the doctrine of karma says that it somehow returns to us to impress on the soul the painful consequences of hate. The pain teaches, and eventually we learn to transform hate into love. The wiser soul, upon putting out an iota of hate, is more sensitive to the pain it is inflicting and puts an iota of love into the world to restore balance and redeem itself. This is common in everyday relations, where we lose our temper, then try to make it up with flowers and caresses. In the reverse, if we put out an iota of love, we get back an iota of love, learning the happy consequences. As the Beatles sang: "In the end the love we take is equal to the love we make."

Central to the doctrine of karma is the growth of the soul, life's lessons. A moral universe puts us in the best arena of life to force the growth of the soul. Thus opportunities and fortunes, as well as challenges and obstacles, become a means for the soul to evolve. It may not appear that way in the short term, but from a cosmic point of view of a soul over many lifetimes, the evolutionary impact of these becomes clearer.

Parananda, a Hindu monk I met during an earlier trip to India in 1986, told me that Tibet was annexed by China because of the Tibetan's karma of practicing black magic. Put simply, black magic is the practice of using spiritual energy for selfish purposes. According to Parananda, this practice had to be weeded out, and the best people to do this were impious Chinese soldiers who destroyed most of the Tibetan monasteries with impunity.

That was the point of view of a Hindu monk. Most Tibetan monks believe that Tibet was annexed because the monasteries, where political power was based in Tibet, became engrossed in internal fighting and power politics, which perhaps amounts to the same thing as black magic. Another common opinion is that the Tibetans had become too isolated and biased against other people and traditions. This caused a need for violent change to force openness and teach the value of diversity. Of course, all of this is speculation. Life is exceedingly complex, and karma, as the Bhagavad-Gita proclaims, is unfathomable.

IN BUDDHISM THERE is a concept called the path of the bodhisattva. This path is centered around the concept of universal compassion and advocates the act of reaching out to help others evolve. There is a Zen story of a wealthy landlady who gave a Buddhist monk a small hut where he could live and engage in his spiritual practices. After twenty years of meditation, the monk was approached one day by a young woman who asked for his affections. His only response was, "I am a cold rock." The landlady kicked him out, remarking that after twenty years, he had learned nothing.

Spirituality is not meant to make people cold rocks. It is meant to melt the rocks of ignorance with spiritual light and compassion. This is the way of the bodhisattva.

The doctrines of reincarnation and karma give a framework for understanding a moral and just universe. But its practical application to everyday life is limited. It is the vision of the future that is more relevant. And this brings us back to the silent inner voice that guides our souls, the bubbling up of thoughts that inspire us and push us forward. The same voice that guides our souls must also guide societies and nations through a collective process. This is what I came to Dharmsala for—to be, in some small way, part of a collective process that looks forward to the future of Tibet.

A Constitution for the Dalai Lama

THE CONSTITUTION REDRAFTING Committee was small: four members (two of whom never came to meetings) and the general secretary, who translated. They were from the old guard who had left Tibet with the Dalai Lama over thirty years earlier. They spoke no English and still held bitter memories about the Chinese. Our first meeting was a welcoming Tibetan luncheon with buttered tea and *momos* (meat wrapped in dough and steamed) and many pleasantries.

We spent the first few days discussing general theories about constitutions. A constitution is a body of laws that "constitute" a government. The idea is that there should be laws that stand above a government, laws that a government is accountable to. The origins of this idea are in religion and "natural law" philosophies that consider life to be subject to a higher divine law. In feudal times, the idea that a "king can do no wrong" was challenged by arguments that kings were subject to divine and natural laws.

Plato proposed that the best government is one headed by a "philosopher king," who was capable of perceiving divine laws and applying them in governing. Tibetan philosophy of government is much like this. Tibetans believe that the Dalai Lama is the incarnation of divine compassion and, as such, incarnates again and again to rule them.

No one knows better than the Dalai Lama how faulty this type of government can be. The system is good in theory but not in practice. Tibetan history is rampant with power struggles between different groups trying to gain influence and power over the Dalai Lama. The committee informed me that the Dalai Lama has thus rejected this system and wants to have no part in a future government of Tibet. He insists on a clear separation between religious institutions and government.

It is good to have enlightened leaders whenever we can find them. But a government consists of more than just leaders. A government is a large organization that has a dynamic relationship with the millions of people it governs. A constitution is needed to define that organization and its relationship with the people.

The American constitution is considered to be the first written constitution of a country. The "founding fathers" were students of natural law philosophy. When Alexander Hamilton was an eighteen-year-old student at King's College (Columbia), he wrote two small but widely distributed pamphlets criticizing the British. He said: "The Sacred Rights of Mankind are not to be rummaged for among old parchments or musty records. They are written, as with a sunbeam, in the whole volume of human nature, by the hand of the Divinity itself, and can never be erased or obscured." (Cousins, Norman. *In God We Trust*. New York: Harper, 1958)

Two years later, Hamilton was appointed aide-de-camp to General George Washington, with the rank of lieutenant colonel. Hamilton was a political prodigy, as Mozart was a musical prodigy. Years later, Dartmouth College gave Hamilton an honorary degree of Doctor of the Laws of Nature and Nations in recognition of his expertise in natural law. Hamilton argued that political life, like individual life, must have something sacred at its foundation or it will devolve into oppression and misery. The Declaration of Independence, signed one year after Hamilton's pamphlets were written, declared life, liberty, and the pursuit of happiness to be natural rights given by the Creator.

The founding fathers did not attempt to make a list of all natural laws. For them, human rights are not given by governments; they were *recognized* by governments as being inherent in human dignity. The Bill of Rights, as the Ninth Amendment implies, was considered to be a limited and inadequate list of natural rights. The constitution as a whole was a practical design for a government that would allow us to pursue these rights as we see them. The nature of these natural rights are only an approximation by society, ever-changing through deliberation.

We tend to think of ourselves as separate from nature. We forget that we evolved the same way as the stars, planets, mountains, and forests; that cultures come and go the same as any other natural occurrences. I think one reason we feel this separation is that we have free will and act for our own interest (not necessarily nature's interest). But if we consider free will to be part of natural evolution, it is also part of nature, and our free will is part of the natural process. Thus the whole grand and often insane march of civilization can be seen as a natural evolutionary process acting to a large extent through our free will.

But consider also that free will makes up only a small part of who we are. Simple things like digestion of food and sense perceptions are independent of our will. This is also true of much of our thought process. Music is often created, not by analytical thought, but by inspiration, a process of drawing on the depths of our being. This is true of all creative thinking, whether it is art, math, science, or problem solving, all of which are instrumental in pushing civilization forward. It is less a linear process than an inner organic flowering experience.

Plato argued that we never really learn things. We remember things that lie dormant inside us. Math, he said, is a natural capability that is awakened in the mind, not imposed on the mind. The creative process comes from something much deeper than the intellect. It is closer to what we would call a natural process. It is a process bubbling up from the same creative power that makes flowers grow and the wind blow. It is the creative process, and more to the point, it is the spiritual process, that anchors us to nature.

Government and law making, like any social event, is part of this evolutionary process. It is often argued that because divine law is eternal and unchanging, it must be the same for everyone. I have always found this reasoning to overlook the great complexity of human life. As we do not always apply the same rules to children as we do to adults, it is easy to see why there may be different laws for different cultures or different laws for people at varying levels of evolution. An evolving society means an evolving governmental and legal system. From this perspective, law and government are meant to change and evolve and are part of the flowering of humanity. This flowering is a collective process of self-discovery and the awakening of society.

I SPENT A few days explaining the American constitution to the Tibetan committee. The American constitution is based on basic principles that can be applied in drafting any constitution. Separation of powers is the most fundamental of these principles. There is the separation of the executive, legislative, and judiciary (the "horizontal" separation) and the separation of the federal and state governments (the "vertical" separation). Separation of powers prevents a concentration and corruption of power.

The founding fathers, like the ancient Greeks, discovered that legislative assemblies could be just as tyrannical as a dictator. The Greeks divided governments into three categories: monarchy, aristocracy, and democracy. Monarchies degenerated into dictatorships, aristocracies into oppressive

oligarchies, and democracies into anarchies. Greek democracies were simply assemblies, often prone to mass hysteria.
Majority rule is not always wise rule. Separation of powers
put a new dimension into democracy.

The emotional whims of assemblies were put in check
by the founding fathers by dividing Congress into two
houses, having a president with the power of veto over
legislation, and establishing an independent judiciary.
George Washington is said to have demonstrated the value
of two houses by pouring hot coffee from a cup into a
saucer and saying that, like the saucer, a second house of
Congress allows hot issues to cool off.

Dictatorial power in the president was prevented by a
Congress that has exclusive power over law making,
including the power to override a veto with a two-thirds
majority vote, and by a Senate that must approve treaties
with a two-thirds majority vote and give its consent to
presidential appointments.

There is another purpose of this division: separate roles.
The role of Congress is to deliberate slowly and thoroughly
in making laws, and the role of the president is to execute
those laws quickly and effectively. It is not good to have
laws pushed through Congress nor to have a president that
hesitates as the ship of state is sinking.

Many countries today have independent commissions,
such as human rights or environmental commissions, that
are further extensions of the principle of the horizontal
separation of powers. Finally, a country vertically divided
into states (federalism) prevents any one region from
dominating the national government. It also ensures that
local issues are dealt with by local governments and not by
a national government far removed from local concerns.

Basic to a constitution are human rights, which define the relationship between government and society. Civil and political rights, such as freedom of speech, press, and assembly, the right to vote, and legal due process, define our rights against the government to protect us from abuse of power. They also ensure the transparency of government so that people can see through it, scrutinize it, and "throw out the bums" if they do not like what they see. Social and economic rights define the duties of the government to ensure, in some way, the health, education, economic, and general welfare of the people.

Thomas Paine's theory that democracy secures human rights is sound in principle. If government is sensitive to the needs of the populace, human rights will emerge and flourish. However, democracies are rarely so sensitive. Constitutional provisions for human rights forces that sensitivity, providing the compassionate eyes of government.

The founding fathers did not think that a constitution by itself could make a good society. James Madison made the famous remark that, if we were all angels, there would be no need for a constitution. On the other hand, if we were all devils, a constitution would not help matters. The founding fathers reasoned that, for a constitution to work, people have to be predominately good. Any constitution can be corrupted if enough people want to corrupt it. A constitution is meant to minimize the influence of corrupting powers, such as special interest groups and big money, and to maximize the creative powers of society. Government does not create culture. It cannot manufacture a Mozart or a Hamilton. But it can provide the protection and sometimes the nourishing environment for culture to flower by its own inherent forces.

These are just bare-bones considerations for a constitution. But for people not familiar with constitutions, like the Tibetans in the committee, it takes some explaining. When I was explaining the concept of presumption of innocence, they protested, saying, "But why would a person be arrested and put on trial if he was presumed innocent?"

During this time, the committee also gave me a clear presentation of what the Tibetans wanted in a constitution. There are countless possible forms for a democracy-based constitution. The Tibetans wanted a presidential form, like the United States has, as opposed to a parliamentary form common in Asia and Europe. But my real challenge as a constitutional adviser was to adapt the constitution to the unique needs and customs of the Tibetan people.

Tibetans have a history of factions struggling for power. The Tibetan community is not uniform, but consists of various divisions made on the basis of religion, region, and family ties. They needed a constitution that will protect them from factional infighting and institutionalize their ideals of compassion and nonviolence.

After these preliminary discussions, we got to work drafting the constitution for Tibet. I would draft, article by article, and dictate to the committee through the interpreter. The committee would ask me a load of questions, scrutinizing each sentence of my answer. Most of the articles were accepted. Occasionally they were changed a bit, and a few were rejected. The process took a couple of months.

The result was a good working constitution. It had a complete bill of rights, an independent human rights commission, and an independent environmental commission. In keeping with the Dalai Lama's vision, there was no military. The Tibetan Buddhist vision was incorporated into the "directive principles," which define the political philosophy of the government: "Compassion is the supreme guiding light of the government of Tibet. Compassion is the most noble virtue of a people and the greatest act of a government. . . . Tibet is a sanctuary of peace. The principle of nonviolence is the cardinal principle of government and the foundation of a civil society. . . . Tibet is a sanctuary of environmental purity. It is the purpose of the government of Tibet to sustain an environment that is pollution free and pristine. . . . The Tibetan economy shall be self-sufficient, shall promote spiritual and moral values, and shall be environmentally friendly."

I tried to find a way to prevent infighting among rival political parties. In India much of the time is spent in political infighting among their parties. As a result, the true business of government is neglected and India seems to have a new government every year. America has its own problems in this area. In the end, the only thing I could think of was a provision prohibiting the legislative body from adopting any rules dealing with political parties. That meant no rules giving majority-party members any special privileges, such as the right to chair committees or to sit in certain seats. I also put a clause in the oath for legislators where they pledged to vote their conscience and not to vote as agents of any organization. These provisions had little teeth in them, but they did give things a nudge away from party politics.

I also put in a provision requiring a two-thirds-majority vote for increasing taxes or incurring debts; a requirement for maintaining a balanced budget, term limits for members of congress, a provision limiting appropriation bills to a single subject to prevent bills from being packed with "pork," and a provision requiring that all legislation be drafted in simple, plain language.

BEFORE I HAD left for this mission, I had contacted a seasoned constitutional adviser by the name of Albert Blaustein. He was known as the "Jewish Madison," because he was an (American) Jew who had helped draft about twenty constitutions for countries like Russia, Brazil, Peru, Nepal, Bangladesh, Niger, and Zimbabwe. He taught at Rutgers University Law School in New Jersey and had taught the only course in the United States on constitutional drafting. I read about him years before and he was one of my inspirations for going to law school. He agreed to review the work I was doing. So when the draft was finished, the committee and I met Professor Blaustein in New Delhi.

Blaustein was even shorter than I am, so the Tibetan's perception of Americans kept being challenged. He was a powerful speaker. When he spoke, the whole room vibrated and the Tibetans listened in awe.

The Tibetans had me draft a constitution for an independent Tibet. Blaustein told the Tibetans that a constitution for an autonomous Tibet within China would be far more practical than one for independence. (Autonomy means a region within a country has its own government and decides issues of local nature, leaving national issues to the national government.) The Tibetans looked at him with stony faces and did not respond. I had floated the idea much earlier but thought the professor would have a better shot at convincing them. We did not raise the issue again.

Blaustein and I went through each article of the constitution in the lounges of five-star hotels, his favorite hangouts. We took out a few things, added a few things, and generally refined the document. While working in a private club in one five-star hotel, Blaustein picked up the newest issue of the *Economist* from a shelf, rolled it up and stuck it into his pocket, saying, "Oh good, I won't have to buy it and I'll save a few bucks." Such idiosyncrasies gave him colorful dimensions. He was a very likable old man prone to telling jokes and making observations on human nature. Every night he would find some party or social event to drag me to, bragging about getting me free meals. One night he addressed the Indian Supreme Court Bar Association and, without any preparation, gave an inspired speech on human rights, filling the room with his booming voice. He was a brilliant adviser.

Some months afterwards he passed away, putting an end to my mentorship and our plans to do similar work for the American Indians and the people of Kurdistan. *Time* magazine, summing up his life in its "Milestone" section, commented that Blaustein had "become something of a founding father to countries around the world." (*Time*. Sept. 5, 1994.)

THE CONSTITUTION BEING done, the committee made arrangements for me to meet the Dalai Lama. It is not easy to get to meet him. He is booked months ahead and is jealously guarded by his private office, which screens those who want to meet him.

The Dalai Lama's legal status in the world is that of a refugee under the protection of the government of India. His compound is protected by Indian soldiers, and Indian intelligence officers monitor all movements around him.

Passing through this outer ring of protection, I entered the silence of his compound that composes his private office and residence. I was dressed in my best suit and tie and carried a white silken scarf. His secretary led me into the Dalai Lama's "audience" room, where, standing to greet me, was a smiling Dalai Lama. I bowed slightly with hands together in front of my chest, as if in prayer, for the customary formal greeting among Tibetans and Indians. Draped over my hands was the scarf, which the Dalai Lama took and then placed around my neck in a ritual blessing he gives to all who come to met him.

The Dalai Lama's eyes were beaming with love. All of my defenses were melted away and I forgot for a moment why I was even there. As we sat, the Dalai Lama's demeanor changed from abstract love to incredible focus of mind. The energy of love that streamed out of his eyes now became an intense energy of inquisitiveness and intelligence. This shocked me back to my normal frame of mind and to the business at hand.

The business was the constitution of Tibet and Tibetan autonomy. He was very upset that the Constitution Redrafting Committee was drafting a constitution for an independent Tibet. He told me in a very forceful tone, "Our policy has been Tibetan autonomy for fifteen years. A constitution for Tibetan autonomy should definitely be done." I was happily surprised. I came into the meeting expecting to argue the case for autonomy but found the Dalai Lama had come to this conclusion fifteen years earlier.

The next issue was a model agreement between the Dalai Lama and Beijing that I wanted to draft. I suggested that such an agreement should be drafted around a type of "Vatican" for the institution of the Dalai Lama. The

Vatican has a status in international law similar to a sovereign state. It is thus protected by international law. I wanted the Dalai Lama to have the same status. At first he resisted the idea, saying that "I do not want anything for myself, just for the Tibetan people." But when I pointed out that a Vatican-based agreement would give Tibetan autonomy international status and protection, he perked up and said, "That is good, that is good."

At the end of the meeting, I took out some beads, showed them to the Dalai Lama and said, "These belong to a friend of mine. She's going through some problems. I wonder if you could bless them." "Yes, yes," he said. He took them with both hands, closed his eyes, chanted some verses in Tibetan, then returned them with a smile. In the Tibetan Buddhist community, having beads blessed by the Dalai Lama is spiritual gold.

As the Dalai Lama walked me out, holding me in his arms, he also took me out of the mental plane and back into that ocean of love that he resides in. He made me feel like the most precious thing on earth. Such love sees all beings as the most precious.

After my meeting, I presented my autonomy projects to the committee and others in his administration. I was surprised to find his administration resisting my autonomy projects as a type of political taboo or plague. The contrast between the Dalai Lama's compassionate, open mind, and the defensive, narrow minds of some in his administration was quite stark. I had innocently expected the administration to accept the Dalai Lama's political policies the same way they accepted his spiritual policies. Their resistance was a slap in the face for me, a violent awakening to politics.

At first I was furious and wanted to crush the resistance. One day during meditation, I saw with my inner eye a large spinning ball of fire. This was my anger. I realized I had lost myself, that I had allowed myself to be overshadowed by the work. It was unprofessional, pointless, and dangerous. When I got my senses back, I dealt with the problem by doing the work on my own, outside of the administration, and having the work submitted directly to the Dalai Lama.

The Chinese Constitution gives a general outline for Tibetan autonomy, but political realities have not allowed it to be implemented. I drafted a constitution that was consistent with the Chinese Constitution but that detailed the particulars of autonomy, such as local powers over culture, education, environment, and human rights.

I was told by a couple of Tibetan friends that because of my support of Tibetan autonomy (versus independence), I should be careful about my physical safety. But other than hearing gossip about my being a CIA agent and unsuccessful attempts by some Tibetan officials to get the Indian government to expel me, I never felt threatened. Most Tibetans remained friendly.

The Dalai Lama has not had an easy life. I always tell people that the Dalai Lama has two problems to deal with: the Chinese and the Tibetans. This is because most people think the problem is only the Chinese. The Chinese problem is, of course, fundamental. When China annexed Tibet in 1951, the fates of both became intertwined. Tibet's first decades under control of the People's Republic of China were marked by political and social turmoil in which millions of lives were lost and families and cultures were destroyed throughout all of China.

Religion was rejected as a competitor to communist ideology, and the Tibetans, for whom religion is the core of their being, fought for their lives. But the reforms under Deng Xiaoping changed the direction of China, and the focus now in China is no longer ideology but economics and, to a degree, democratization.

I often heard Tibetans speak of the "right" to independence. There are certain legal arguments that can be made for and against such a right. But these are all academic. Currently, no country in the world recognizes the right of Tibetan independence, which makes independence impossible. However, independence is not necessary to fulfill the interests of the Tibetans.

The international community gives its full support for the promotion of democracy and human rights. Understanding this, the Dalai Lama promotes a policy he calls the "middle-way approach," which accepts Chinese sovereignty over Tibet but promotes cultural autonomy, democracy, and human rights. The Dalai Lama is not concerned with antiquated ideas of sovereignty but with the welfare of the Tibetan people.

The Dalai Lama's policy is wise. But selling it is not simply a matter of convincing people of its wisdom. The resistance is not on a rational level, but on an emotional one. I remember a girlfriend of mine who had been raped some years before I met her. She periodically had nightmares from this experience. After we had lived together and slept in the same bed for a while, her nightmares stopped and never returned. The love in the relationship created a healing influence. It would be of little help if I told her simply that past is past and just forget about it. The wound was not on that level. Love was the remedy, not reason.

Tibetans carry deep emotional wounds either from direct experience or through the memories of relatives and friends, creating a cultural memory. These memories are kept alive, and thus the fires of animosity are kept burning, exploding in protests and calls for independence. On top of this is a wall of suspicion and mistrust between the Tibetans and Chinese that has been built over the decades. In attempting to reconcile the Tibetans with the Chinese, the Dalai Lama has to be the healer; he has to heal these emotional wounds with words of compassion. It is fitting that the Dalai Lama is both a political leader and a high priest.

Beijing

WHILE IN DHARMSALA, I had a vision of the Dalai Lama during meditation. He was beaming with eyes of joy and presenting me with gold to take to Beijing. This had little to do with the real-life Dalai Lama, except that we shared the same desire for better relations between the Chinese and the Tibetans. The vision was a welling up of my own consciousness, seeds of desire and purpose sprouting from my soul. I had not thought of doing anything along these lines, and my experiences in Dharmsala had washed the fires of inspiration away, but this vision rekindled an interest in the Tibet issue.

At that time (1994), the Tibetan parliament in Dharmsala had a resolution prohibiting the Tibetan administration from approaching China to open a dialogue. If China came forward, the Tibetan administration would consider talks, but they would not go forward themselves. This prohibition did not apply to the Dalai Lama or to third parties. The chairman of the parliament, Samdhong Rinpoche, encouraged me (as a third party) to see what I could do to open up a dialogue. The Rinpoche had little hope that a dialogue would emerge. But I was so enthusiastic about the possibility that he thought he'd let me run with the idea to see where it led. He was always open to possibilities.

When I first met Samdhong Rinpoche, I thought I was looking at a Mayan Indian. Tibetans often resemble American Indians and are sometimes mistaken for them. The cultures are also similar. Peter Gold, an anthropologist I met in Dharmsala, wrote a book on the subject called *Navajo & Tibetan Sacred Wisdom.*

I knew Samdhong Rinpoche from the Constitution Redrafting Committee. He was a member but had been too busy to attend meetings. I kept him informed as the work progressed in the committee, and it was to him that I gave my finished products on Tibetan autonomy for presentation to the Dalai Lama. The Rinpoche, constitutionally, was the highest official of the administration under the Dalai Lama. The Kashag, the executive branch of the administration, was accountable to the parliament and could be removed by it. As chairman of the parliament, the Rinpoche was constantly trying to balance competing interests, particularly regarding the policy division between autonomy and independence.

This was my first attempt at mediation, so I decided on a conservative approach. Instead of going to Beijing directly, I solicited governments to facilitate a dialogue. This put the issue in the hands of career diplomats. I approached governments through their embassies in New Delhi. Because the Dalai Lama is based in India, most embassies there had diplomats that followed the Tibet issue. I approached the embassies of the United States, Germany,

France, Australia, Canada, Sweden, and Mongolia.

My first order of business was to clarify the Dalai Lama's policy of "middle-way approach." The media was full of statements by Tibetans and Tibet support groups in the West promoting "free Tibet," or independence. The result was confusion. Many people, including diplomats, thought that the Dalai Lama sought Tibetan independence. In some cases, I had to bring the Rinpoche to meetings so that he could confirm on record that the Dalai Lama was willing to accept Chinese sovereignty.

This clarification was immensely important. First, it revealed that the Dalai Lama's policy was consistent with China's own policy of Chinese sovereignty over Tibet. Second, with this clarification, diplomats, on their own initiative, could bring the issue up in meetings with the Chinese. The Chinese, convinced that the Dalai Lama was a "splittist," needed constant reminders that he was not.

All of these countries were willing to help through their normal diplomatic channels whenever the issue of Tibet arose with the Chinese. Two countries, Mongolia and Sweden, agreed to make special efforts. Mongolia especially had an interest because its main religion was Tibetan Buddhism.

Arrangements were made through the Rinpoche for these diplomats to meet with the Dalai Lama. The Swedes had some difficulty when they spoke with the Dalai Lama's Kashag. The Kashag, unaware of my efforts and the substance of the meetings, gave a presentation to the Swedish diplomats that was fully at odds with the Dalai Lama's policy. I explained the problem to the Swedes, pointing out that the Dalai Lama was the final authority on the issue of talks with the Chinese. The final results were agreements with the Dalai Lama by Sweden and Mongolia to actively aid in opening a dialogue with the Chinese.

I spent many hours in talks with the Mongolian ambassador. He spoke with a soft voice and the deep wisdom of Asia. The peace process, he told me, would take a decade or longer. Typical of a Westerner, I thought in terms of months and did not fully appreciate the ambassador's insight. The Swedes and Mongolians tried their best, but the Chinese did not respond well. The Chinese were not convinced of the sincerity of the Tibetans. But it must have helped. Every time a diplomat brought up the issue of the Dalai Lama to the Chinese, it reinforced the point that the Tibet issue was important to the international community and that the Dalai Lama's policy was reasonable.

I DECIDED TO go to Beijing to see for myself whether anything was possible. Before I left, I saw a famous lama in Kathmandu by the name of Kapatri Rinpoche. He was unusual for a Tibetan because he had a long beard. In fact, he is the only Tibetan I can remember with a beard. (Tibetans have little facial hair.) I asked him whether a trip to Beijing would be of value to promote reconciliation. He did mo (divination) on the question and said it was a great idea. He also recommended a *Tara* puja to remove obstacles in the trip, and I arranged for his monastery in the hills north of Kathmandu to do the ceremony. Tara is a Tibetan form of Mother Divine, and these pujas are thought to infuse spiritual energy into the person's endeavors.

This was a way for me to allow the Tibetan culture to participate in my work. It was, after all, for their benefit. I found the Tibetan politicians to be somewhat corrupt and insincere, but I found working with the monks to be easy. Samdhong Rinpoche was a monk as well as a politician, which is probably why we got along. So with Samdhong's and Kapatri's blessings, I arrived in Beijing in the early spring of 1995.

Beijing is a beautiful city, clean, orderly, and bustling with business, from large corporate activity to small vendors selling baked sweet potatoes cooked and sold on the side of the street. One day I met a Tibetan nomad with matted hair, clad in traditional clothing, walking the streets selling large Tibetan knives.

Being on a low budget, I found a dormitory room at the University of Nationalities. Most universities have special dormitories for foreign students who are learning Chinese or who are engaged in some other academic pursuit. My room turned out to be convenient, because the University of Nationalities, as the title suggests, was established for the many nationalities (ethnic minorities) in China, including Tibetans. There was an Institute of Tibetology at the university, and I met with its director the day after I arrived.

The director was Tibetan, and he was thrilled that an American had come to discuss the Tibet issue. He knew of Samdhong Rinpoche by his reputation as a Sanskrit scholar and as the director of the Institute of Higher Tibetan Studies in India. I suggested that the Rinpoche could come as a visiting lecturer and could engage in informal talks with Chinese officials while here. This would provide a way to have talks without the formalities, a way to break the ice. He liked the idea and contacted the "authorities."

The next day I met with these authorities: the director and staff from the office of foreign relations for the City of Beijing. The university was under the city government, and his office dealt with foreigners visiting the city. The meeting went on for a couple of hours. I emphasized the point that the Dalai Lama was willing to accept Tibet as part of China. The director told me he had read reports of the Dalai Lama stating that Tibet would be better off economically if it remained part of China. However, then he added, "But let us see if he is sincere." The suspicion was thick.

Afterwards the director and his staff took me out for Peking duck at a fancy restaurant and we dined in a private room. The director brought up Tiananmen Square and compared it to the 1965 Los Angeles Watts riots, saying that he was there and had seen people gunned down by "Marines." I doubted his testimony and thought Kent State was a better analogy, but did not mention it. I have a policy of avoiding battles that are not relevant to the business at hand. I just responded, "Well, there is much misunderstanding between our cultures" and went on to other things.

After lunch, the translator, a lovely young lady with a sweet accent, and a young man from security, took me to the Summer Palace for sight-seeing. Among the many sights was a Tibetan Buddhist temple. It was a long, happy day.

Government structure in China is a little confusing. The Chinese Communist Party permeates the government. This means government decisions and party decisions are intertwined. The director told me he would present my proposal to their "leaders," which meant the leadership of the party. The American first secretary (political section) at the U.S. embassy in Beijing told me he thought this would go all the way to the top, meaning the Politburo. Anyway, it took ten days for an answer to come back.

The answer was twofold. The Rinpoche, according to their intelligence, was a "separatist," and relations were not "mature" enough for even informal talks. The translator, in a sweet and sympathetic tone said, "I'm sorry, it's just so hard for them to change." This was very courageous for her to admit, considering that she was surely being recorded. I responded, "I understand, the Tibetans are just as stubborn." I defended the Rinpoche, saying that he was the Tibetan's biggest supporter of the Dalai Lama's middle-way approach. But this had little effect. They had to rely on their own intelligence reports. I countered with other proposals, and we went back and forth for a while.

In the end, the Chinese told me that relations should proceed through the principle of "proportionate reciprocity." The Chinese would respond "in equal proportion" to any conciliatory act made by the Dalai Lama. The Chinese wanted the Dalai Lama to accept Tibet as part of China and end "separatist activity," especially in Tibet. Anything in this direction would result in a positive response from their side, in particular the opening of dialogue. The Chinese asked me to convey this to the Dalai Lama.

Reciprocity was fundamental to their relations with foreign nations, especially the United States. There was no reason to doubt their sincerity. Their insistence that the Dalai Lama come forward first is a matter of protocol. Perhaps it stems from their Confucian perspective: Beijing is the "father" figure, and the Dalai Lama the "son." The son must come forward first. This simple formula was the fruit of my efforts. I was satisfied with it. It was practical and something that could work.

I WAS IN Beijing for about two months. The meetings took little time, so much of my time was spent getting to know Beijing and the Chinese. Central to mediation and diplomacy is respect. Respect is the universal currency, the channel by which dialogue becomes possible. Respect means appreciation, and this means getting to know the culture and people. I spent much time befriending students, professors, and locals.

I spent many days wandering the streets of Beijing. I visited a Tibetan Buddhist monastery with monks from Mongolia. I also toured ancient streets and buildings and numerous parks. In the mornings, the parks were full of people practicing tai chi, and during the day, they were full of colorful flying kites. The Chinese took park-going seriously and always dressed well when they went. Dress in Beijing has changed since the days of the blue Mao uniform. Taxi drivers wear suit jackets (without tie) and military women wear stylized uniforms with high heels, stockings, and makeup.

I visited an important Tibetan in Beijing by the name of Phontsok Wangyal. Phontsok was the first communist Tibetan and acted as a translator between the Dalai Lama and the Chinese when the Chinese first came to Tibet in the 1950s. During the cultural revolution, he was imprisoned like so many others. He was now a senior adviser on Tibetan issues to China's National Assembly (their congress). His apartment was full of Tibetan rugs and tankas and the familiar aroma of Tibetan incense. His niece, visiting from Tibet, served us hot Tibetan tea, full of butter. She was a nun with those bright red cheeks common among Tibetan woman. Phontsok was happy to see me, telling me, "The conflict is destroying Tibet. Something must be done soon or it will be too late."

Phontsok had written a book claiming there was water on the moon. The claim was based on an esoteric system of analysis I found difficult to understand. He was extremely proud of it and had sent a copy to the Dalai Lama. I did not see the significance of his claim, until later when a NASA probe provided good evidence that there is water on the moon. NASA claimed this would make a moon station much easier because water and oxygen would not have to be transported to the moon from Earth. This evidence must have boosted the sale of Phontsok's book.

A PROFESSOR I got to know was a master of *chi gong*, the mystical teachings of Taoism. Tai chi is one of the many practices of chi gong. Chi gong, like most mystical systems, describes the universe as composed of levels of energy. The physical level is the outermost. Permeating the physical creation is the "etheric" or "vital" level. The human body is composed of a physical level and an etheric level.

It is, supposedly, the etheric energy of the body where sensation resides. Local anesthesia has the effect of pushing the etheric body away from the particular part of the physical body so that pain is not felt. When the arm or leg falls asleep, the etheric body becomes out of phase with the physical. And when one drinks alcohol (an anesthetic), the etheric brain (where it is said memory is stored) comes out-of-phase with the physical brain, making one relaxed and mentally out-of-phase. There are physiological explanations for all this, of course, but this is the mystical explanation.

The etheric body is said to be a matrix of energy that governs the general functioning of the body: digestion, assimilation, and growth. It coordinates the billions of operations happening throughout the body that we are generally unaware of. In chi gong, the healer, using acupuncture and other techniques, operates mainly on the etheric level, restoring the relationship between the etheric energy and body, getting them working together.

Above the etheric levels are the energy fields that compose emotions and mental activity. The lower levels compose primal emotions and thoughts; the higher levels compose the higher dimensions of love and wisdom. At the highest and finest levels of love and wisdom, we reach the universal source of energy—the eternal shores of pure Spirit.

The professor I befriended did practices that channel energy in various circles through and around his body. Sitting with the professor in his dormitory room, I watched him close his eyes and say something like, "Now I am the wind" or "Now I am the ocean." I would feel this energy flowing through the room. His bookshelves were full of books on chi gong with unmarked bookcovers to avoid the critical eyes of some of his associates at the university.

Chi gong is a central source of the concept of "The Force" in the *Star Wars* movies. The connection is revealed in the name of Jedi master Qui-Gon in episode one, a play on the term chi gong. George Lucas was looking for a way to portray a spiritual philosophy that was common to all traditions. Taoism, with its simplicity and lack of religious trappings, fulfilled that need. Chi gong is also the mystical foundation for kung fu, which plays into the concept of the Jedi Knight. The light-saber is borrowed from the samurai sword, and the art form for wielding the light-saber from the samurai tradition of Japan. The legendary samurai

Miyamoto Musashi, in his *Book of Five Rings*, places the Zen Buddhist ideal of emptiness or inner peace and silence, as the foundation of the samurai's strength and skill.

There are also elements of the Jedi Knight in the Knights of the Holy Grail and in Gandalf, the wizard, who overcomes the Lord of Darkness in J. R. R. Tolkien's *Lord of the Rings*. Like the Grail Knights and Gandalf, the Jedi Knight combines the priest, politician, and soldier into one personality, as a guardian of human society. The Dalai Lama represents the manifestation of this archetype in the real world. However, rather than fighting with the sword, the Dalai Lama "fights" with love. This is a central reason why he was awarded the Nobel Peace Prize.

A central theme of the Lucas mythology is the nature of evil. This is also a central consideration for a peacemaker: What is evil? Where does it come from, and how is it destroyed? There were a few occasions many years ago when I would have a dream of facing a lord of darkness. In the dreams, I knew I could not win in a physical fight with him, but stood my ground nevertheless, awakening in a cold sweat. The dreams humbled me and reminded me of how limited my power was. The lord of darkness is only a symbol of evil in the world. He is not real. Above the human level, in the realm of angels and archangels, I suspect there is no evil. Such beings are too evolved. Evil is peculiar to humans, with our underdeveloped minds and coarse desires. Evil is a mirror image of our own inadequacies.

In chi gong, as in other spiritual disciplines, physiological, psychological, and spiritual health are seen as a proper coordination between the various levels that make up a person, beginning with the physical body and ending at the shores of the divine. Evil occurs when the lower levels of a person are cut asunder from the higher levels (usually by overwhelming desire and passion), casting the person adrift with no guide or conscience. The true healer can restore this connection, bringing spiritual health.

Evil is not inherent in humans but is foreign. In episode one of *Star Wars*, Anakin Skywalker, (who later grows up to become the evil Darth Vader) is portrayed as an innocent child. He is exceptionally good-natured and seeks to help others with no thought of reward. It all begins with innocence. Somehow in the storms of life, the innocence is clouded, and the connection to the higher impulses is cut off. The lower self retains its abilities but has lost its connection with the spiritual light and follows a path of darkness that can lead only to death and destruction.

Thus are created the "Hitler" and the "mad scientist," who have great skill and intellectual abilities but no wisdom. Anakin Skywalker is even more dangerous, because he has not only skill and high mental abilities, but also occult powers. But Anakin is redeemed in the end of *The Return of the Jedi*. There was still good in him, and his son, Luke, was able to draw it out, reconnecting him to his "true" self.

There is a beautiful metaphor in the Upanishads of two birds in the tree of life. One eats the fruit, the other does not, but only looks on. The two birds represent the higher and lower aspects of our selves. The higher aspect, the bird that does not eat the fruit, is the divine spark that is never touched, always retaining its purity. The lower aspect, the bird that eats the fruit, is the personality that enters the world of experience, to learn and grow.

The wisdom the personality accumulates through experience is absorbed by the higher divine self that remains untainted and pure, beyond the corrupting influence of the world. This purity, although at times overshadowed, is never corrupted. Over time this divine purity—the true innocence—will bring the lower personality back into alignment with the path of light.

We all suffer the fall and redemption of Anakin Skywalker to some degree, losing our senses, getting caught up in a web of illusions, then finding ourselves again. The great "fall" is the incarnation of the soul into the world of experiences; the great "redemption," the union of the soul, perfected after innumerable lifetimes, with God.

Professor Thomas Buergenthal, the director of my LLM program at George Washington University, is a leading scholar in human rights. When he was an eight-year-old child, he was put in a Nazi concentration camp called Birkenau in Poland. He came face to face with evil at a young age. In his work as a human rights scholar he served on the UN Truth Commission to El Salvador, which investigated the atrocities committed during the civil war there. Buergenthal points out that people who commit evil acts are usually "common, ordinary people." Something like a "short circuit in the brain" occurs that convinces them of the rightness of their actions, or simply blinds them completely.

Buergenthal tells a story of a Salvadoran colonel who led a group of military officials in reading scripture and prayer, then ordered the execution of Jesuit priests. They put so much energy into convincing themselves of their rightness, that they blocked out their higher impulses.

In the movie *Kundun*, the Dalai Lama is seen remarking that he thought the Chinese would all have horns but realized upon meeting them that they were just like Tibetans. And yet, consumed by Maoism, the Chinese officials of that time ended up devastating Tibet and China. The Dalai Lama, as the healer, has been working to reconnect his people and the Chinese to the higher impulse ever since.

THE PROFESSOR IN Beijing was curious about my own spiritual practices. Because he practiced circulating energy, he thought I must also practice something similar. I told him that I never experienced circulating energy, only *radiating* energy. He found that fascinating. It was completely foreign to him.

There are a great variety of spiritual practices in the world. As Taoists say, these practices are like the many paths at the base of a mountain that lead up to the same summit. People often ask me what practice is best. I do not think there is a best practice. It's very personal.

The Mongolian ambassador in New Delhi, who had helped in trying to open a dialogue between the Dalai Lama and Beijing, told me that he preferred the Christian tradition to the Buddhist. The reason for this was that the Christian tradition focuses on faith in God to guide our souls and lead us to salvation, whereas the Buddhist tradition places all responsibility on the shoulders of the individual. The ambassador lived through a horrendous time in Mongolia when it was enslaved by the Soviet Union. He told me he felt intuitively that only a higher power could guide him through such times and liberate Mongolia and its people. So even though his country was Buddhist, he preferred the prayers of Christianity over the meditations of Buddhism. It fit his deeply felt needs.

It is often said that a sincere prayer will always be

answered. It may not be in the way we expect or wish. Some people may see the heavens open, and the answer written in the sky. For most, I think, prayers are often answered in a moment of mental clarity. The higher power trickles down, awakening our awareness.

Prayer has the tendency of making us sensitive to a higher power, instilling faith. It is generally said that the highest prayer is not in asking something from God but in surrendering to God, riding on a flow of love to God. The reason is that God must have better plans for us than we can ever possibly imagine. So the real purpose should be in developing an intimacy with the higher life. But during times of darkness, this is not easy. We reach out for an answer, full of tears and anxiety. Faith helps us through the storm to find peace at the end. This is what the Mongolian ambassador sought: deep faith in a higher power that directs our lives.

The Buddha placed emphasis on individual responsibility; Christ placed it on faith in God. They are not exclusive of each other. The Buddha recognized a higher divine power, and Christ acknowledged the value of individual responsibility. It is a matter of emphasis, and a person is drawn to one or the other according to need.

If we consider the soul as an evolving entity over the eternity of time, then all experiences in life contribute to the growth of the soul and thus to spiritual growth. However, "spiritual" is generally considered to begin with the flowering of love, love being the bond connecting us to the higher life. The spiritual path therefore is meant to facilitate this connection, and it involves great transformation. Spiritual development involves every aspect of life, not just a practice. But a practice is meant to give direction; it plugs us into the inner force that transforms and ignites.

According to legend, Buddha gained enlightenment by meditating on the inward and outward flow of his breath. This may be more symbolic than actual: the Buddha found divinity resonating in the depths of his own being. As the Trappist monk Father Thomas Keating has pointed out, meditation is a universal practice. In meditation, any word, phrase, or image can be used that invokes the idea of sacredness and holiness. Sitting with eyes closed, the word is thought in a soft, effortless way. The idea is to allow the mind to fall into its own depths, surrendering to God. God is beyond the narrow boundaries of human thought. Meditation and prayer take us beyond those boundaries, and like a lover putting the mind aside, the soul falls into the arms of the divine in loving embrace. This is the eternal love story of Cupid, the god of love and Psyche, the soul.

In meditation and silent prayer, people often experience great turmoil: storms and whirlpools of feeling and thought. It is often not the peace people associate with the practice. This turmoil is the transforming and healing energy being released, the fires of purification. Inner peace is the fruit of meditation, and often comes afterwards. The common sense way to judge the value of a practice is to see how you feel afterwards. When I first started the practice of meditation, I would meditate for hours. But I felt dull and lethargic afterwards. So I cut it down to about half an hour. You have to play around and find what is best for you and be open to change.

The spiritual path should be playful, not strict and rigid like the army or a bureaucracy. We are ultimately responsible for our own spiritual development, our own relation with God. I've always had an inclination toward silent meditation, perhaps because I was a monk in the past. But I do not try to convince people that they should practice it. Central to spirituality is learning to find your own path.

IF THERE IS a strong desire for spiritual growth, the path tends to show itself. What is fundamental to spiritual life, as in all life, is change, transformation. To grow, a person must be willing to change. Many people embrace spirituality but then resist any form of change in their daily lives. They get on the road and then sit down, going nowhere.

The most fundamental source of spiritual transformation is the silent voice we all have inside. This is the source of all true wisdom. Being sensitive to our thoughts and feelings and to our reactions to experiences in daily life is a way of becoming sensitive to our silent voice. We all have inside us a type of quality-control system; a system of self-purification and self-improvement; an inner force of healing and transformation. If we are sensitive to it and allow it to express itself, we grow. If we drown it out under the passions of desire and egoism, we will not grow.

I'm am not referring to being self-conscious; of being in constant fear and doubt about one's actions. This just leads to anxiety and paralysis of action. I'm referring to being sensitive and aware of one's inner life, often neglected in the flurry of living. People talk of an inner "voice" because it communicates to them. But it is not literally a voice. It is much too subtle. It is more of a knowingness, a nudging, a faint impulse, though it may sometimes shout like a crack of thunder.

People who are close to one another may communicate without speaking, with perhaps facial expressions or just a twinkle of the eye. The inner voice is the depths of one's self communicating with one's more shallow self: the divine trickling down into the soul. The intimacy between one's self and one's inner voice is much closer than that of two friends or lovers. Thus the inner voice is sometimes hardly perceptible, because it is the emergence of the most subtle and refined aspect of one's own nature.

Socrates spoke of an inner voice that said only one thing: "no." If he was about to do something and the voice said "no," he knew from experience to follow the advice. Otherwise, if the voice did not speak, he knew his actions were right. Others have more subtle or more elaborate communications. I think it is very personal.

My earliest memory of this inner correcting force was when I was about four years old and living in the countryside of Georgia. I was standing with some other boys on a hot and dusty dirt road when a school bus full of African-American children came by. One of the boys suggested that, as the bus went by, we all shout the word "nigger." When we did this, my eyes locked into the eyes of an African-American boy, not much older than myself. In his large eyes was a mixture of wonder and hurt. He seemed very close to me, like a brother. I was hit by a thunderbolt, instantly feeling that I had done something wrong. That was the first and last time I ever used the word. No one in my family ever used the word, and no one had told me it was a bad word. I did not understand what had happened, but that inner force understood. It instructed little four-year-old Roger and he obeyed.

Beginning with the vision of the Dalai Lama I had a year earlier, I followed my silent inner voice through political minefields: through deceit, insincerity, and falsehoods. The Tibet issue is so emotionally charged that it created a curtain of illusion. The basic skill of a mediator is to cut through the facades to see the true forces behind a conflict. This took time.

The most common spiritual path is the path of action, where we are constantly testing our thoughts and feelings against reality. Here we purify ourselves in the fires of trial and error. Here we learn slowly and often painfully what inner impulses are false and what inner impulses are true.

In this respect, my experience on the Tibet issue was a type of training camp. By trying to help the Tibetans, I was also helping myself, purifying my thinking and feeling. I do not think I passed with flying colors. But I passed. And I got the prize at the end of my endeavors: a simple key to reconciliation.

In my vision of the Dalai Lama, the gold he presented to me was symbolic, I think, of a spiritual energy to be conveyed to the Chinese. In diplomacy, this is known as sending "good-will." It is something I had to carry in my own heart and mind. The Chinese response did not shine as brightly. It was a faint reflection of what the Dalai Lama offered in the vision. But it glittered nonetheless. With "prize" in hand, I made my way back to the Rinpoche.

Path to Reconciliation

AFTER SOME PROBLEMS (a story told later), I made it to Sarnath, India, and briefed Samdhong Rinpoche. My recommendation was that the Dalai Lama should begin a process of reconciliation by calling for an end to "separatist" activities inside Tibet. The bulk of this activity is carried out by monks and nuns who worship the Dalai

Lama and who would respond to his requests to change. This recommendation was based on a statement given to me from the Chinese leaders that they wanted "action, not words" from the Dalai Lama, and that the main obstacle to talks was "separatist" activity.

Monasteries are traditionally the political sources of power in the Tibetan Autonomous Region (TAR) of China, and the association between religion and politics is still very strong. This is the prime cause for religious repression. China's concern is not with religious practices but with the political activity tied to them. The current Chinese repression of the Falun Gong spiritual organization is not aimed at the practice of chi gong, still freely practiced in China, but at an organization they (wrongly) perceive as threatening their rule. In Tibetan areas in China outside the TAR, Tibetans are not involved in protests. They practice their religion freely, put up pictures of the Dalai Lama at their altars (currently banned inside the TAR), and otherwise enjoy considerable freedom. This fact was clear evidence of China's principle of "proportionate reciprocity" in action: when Tibetans do not protest for independence, the Chinese tend to give more freedom.

Many protests in the TAR are artificially encouraged by Tibetans in exile. This creates an ugly cycle: Tibetans in exile encourage protests inside Tibet, thus leading to repression of protesters and human rights abuses. This leads to Tibetans in exile seeking international support to condemn Chinese repression in Tibet. It was insane. It was important that this cycle be reversed.

I further recommended to the Rinpoche that after a positive response by the Chinese, the Dalai Lama should make a clear statement accepting Tibet as part of China.

The Dalai Lama's position at that time was that "we do not ask for independence." This was an indirect way of accepting Tibet as part of China. But statements by his officials indicating that independence was still pursued, and statements by the Dalai Lama that he was "willing" to accept Tibet as part of China (meaning not yet, but maybe in the future) made his position unclear to the Chinese.

These were just recommendations. The important point was that the path to reconciliation was through a process of proportionate reciprocity, and the Dalai Lama could initiate the process at any time by some variation of the above acts. The Rinpoche was open to the suggestion but, as usual, was cynical about anything happening.

With the Rinpoche's blessings, I headed for Dharmsala to make a presentation to the Dalai Lama. Dharmsala was not very friendly when I arrived. I had met the Dalai Lama's brother, Gyalop Dundub, in Hong Kong before going to Beijing. He had been the liaison between the Dalai Lama and Beijing for many years but had, in his own words, "retired" from this work and wanted no more involvement in the issue. I met him as a matter of courtesy to share my thoughts and to listen to any advice he might have.

He was very friendly to me at the time and discussed the history of talks, specifically the many times that the Tibetans had derailed the peace process every time talks began. When he later visited Dharmsala, he told everyone that I had gone to Beijing to replace him with Samdhong Rinpoche as the liaison between the Dalai Lama and Beijing. This was an act of professional jealousy and created a lot of gossip in Dharmsala. When I arrived, the political atmosphere was poisoned by suspicion.

The Rinpoche was looked on as someone attempting to grab more power by developing a secret relationship with Beijing. His hands were tied and he could not arrange a direct meeting between me and the Dalai Lama. Groupings into political camps and internal infighting is one of the biggest problems with the Tibetans.

I met with the Dalai Lama's political secretary and made my presentation. He told me: "Our position is that the time is not right for opening talks with the Chinese." That infuriated me. "Who is 'our'?" I asked. He fumbled with that question, giving a vague and, I thought, inadequate answer. Whatever "our" meant, it did not include the Dalai Lama. The Dalai Lama's public position was that he was willing to meet with the Chinese anywhere, anytime. Everyone knew that.

I asked a friend of mine, Tulku Daboom, if he could find out what was going on in the Dalai Lama's private office. Daboom was a "nonpolitical" lama. But he had a close friend who was head of the Dalai Lama's private office. When Daboom asked his friend about talks with China, he responded that he did not want the Dalai Lama to "go down in history as the Dalai Lama that gave Tibet away to China." I knew about the resistance to the Dalai Lama's policy but was surprised by how much it extended into his private office.

I vented my frustrations on the Rinpoche, saying, "It's not the Chinese, it's the division among the Tibetans that prevents talks from happening!" I was burned out after two years in Asia, and I was losing my composure. The Rinpoche first denied that there was a division, but then laughed in agreement with me when I said that the division was as clear to me as being hit in the face with a brick. He told me that the Dalai Lama could put an end to separatist activity in Tibet and make a public statement that Tibet is part of China, but only if he got a clear guarantee from China at the highest level that they would respond proportionately. He needed this to justify his actions to the opposition.

On my return to the United States, I stopped over in Beijing and met my Chinese friends on Christmas day at the Jiangua Hotel, just a few blocks from the U.S. embassy. I was trying to get some sympathy from them on the Dalai Lama's problems with his administration. A few days later, I received the message from their "leaders" that this was not their problem; the "Dalai Lama must get his own house in order." They reiterated that if the Dalai Lama responded in a "sincere" manner, they would respond proportionately. They considered this to be clear. Indeed, they had made public statements saying that the main obstacle to talks were separatist activities.

At this point, there was not much more I could do. What was needed was a concerted effort to get support for the Dalai Lama's policy from influential Tibetans and Western support groups. This would be a huge lobbying effort far beyond my abilities as a single mediator. And I was exhausted.

My last act was to draft a public statement. At least I should share my experiences with the public, and perhaps others would pick up where I left off. Not everyone was receptive to what I had to say. For many, I was telling them what they did not want to hear: that the problem was with the Tibetans not the Chinese, that it was the division among Tibetans on policy that prevented dialogue and positive democratic change in Tibet. The Tibetans especially did not want to hear this.

The media was so engrossed in simplistic images of the Chinese as evil and the Tibetans as saintly victims, that my message was an assault on the sacred. One fellow from Associated Press in Beijing told me that to print my story would be to act as a tool for Chinese propaganda. This guy was even more burned out than I was. But for others, such as the diplomatic community, my story was corroboration of their own experiences.

SINCE JANUARY 1996, when I returned to the United States, stories of the division between hard-liners and moderates around the Dalai Lama have surfaced in the media, making the Tibetans more sensitive to the problem. Just before President Clinton went to China in 1998, I talked to the State Department's special coordinator for Tibet, who told me that he emphasized to the Dalai Lama that the Tibetans were still sending China "mixed signals" about Tibetan independence. He also told me that he was not altogether convinced of the sincerity of the Tibetan administration's backing of the Dalai Lama's middle-way policy.

When Clinton went to China and brought up the Tibet issue, President Jiang Zemin said they would be open to a dialogue if the Dalai Lama made a public statement accepting Tibet as part of China. The Tibetans responded positively, claiming that Beijing had become more conciliatory. In actuality, the Chinese position has not changed. It remains the same as when I visited: proportionate reciprocity.

It is the Tibetans who have become more conciliatory. Leaders of the Dalai Lama's administration seem to be getting behind the Dalai Lama's policy for reconciliation. This is the result of an evolutionary process within the

Dalai Lama's administration brought about by inner and outer pressures. But it is still a struggle. As of this writing, no statement has been made from the Dalai Lama's side to begin a process.

I often use the Chinese finger puzzle to demonstrate Chinese policy on Tibet. The puzzle is a small tube woven out of straw. If you put a finger inside each end of the tube and then pull them apart, the tube tightens around the fingers, keeping them tightly inside. To release the fingers, you must bring the fingers together so that the tube loosens its grip. For Tibetans to enjoy freedom inside Tibet, they must come together with the Chinese. Trying to separate themselves from the Chinese only makes the Chinese tighten their grip. The important things for Tibetans are religious and cultural freedom, human rights, and democracy. Over time, this may all be developed within China.

It is easy to find fault with China, especially in the area of human rights. But for every fault we might find (and there are many), we can also find positive developments, such as elections at the village level, and the growing accountability of government officials in their courts. The Chinese people have not forgotten about the ancient Chinese doctrine, "Mandate of Heaven," that considers governments to be accountable to a supreme moral force (Heaven). China's leaders understand that China must change or fall. There is a famous Taoist allegory of the tree that bends with the wind to survive. China must bend to the powerful winds of the changing thinking of its people and the world, or it will collapse.

But China's leaders also fear that changing too fast in a nation of 1.2 billion people may result in anarchy, becoming like leaves scattered by the wind. Thus progress is frustratingly slow, often by a three-steps-forward, two-steps-back process. But it is there to embrace. The prevailing winds of change in China are toward democracy and a federal system where provinces and regions like Tibet will enjoy considerable autonomy. Tibet should be in the forefront of these changes, not behind them, as has been the case for the last two decades.

The path to reconciliation between China and the Tibetans is crystal clear. The Dalai Lama must put an end to the issue of independence, to be reciprocated by the Chinese inviting him back to Tibet to contribute in the democratization process now emerging in China. Tibetan autonomy cannot be created in one day through one agreement. It can only be created through a long process of incremental changes that slowly build trust and harmony between the Tibetans and the Chinese.

If the Tibetans continue as they have in the past to indulge in China bashing, invoking the darker emotions of animosity, then the quagmire will continue. But if they approach the problem from a purely Buddhist point of compassion and "middle way," as the Dalai Lama does, then they can solve their problems with the Chinese. This is the big lesson. It is a spiritual lesson of rising above the darker emotions of suspicion and anger and embracing the higher emotions of compassion and love.

3

KASHMIR

*Disciple: A blue woman appeared to me in
          meditation; the earth quaked! And my
          hair stood on end!*

*Master: The future casts its image on pure
         hearts. Mother Divine is stepping into
         the world.*

New Delhi

THE TWELFTH-CENTURY historical work *River of Kings*
traces the history of Kashmir to the times of the great epic
Mahabharata five thousand years ago. There it is written
that the first king of Kashmir was killed on the battlefield
by Lord Krishna. The symbology is significant. Lord
Krishna, the incarnation of God, came to earth to destroy
wickedness and restore righteousness. Those killed by
Krishna are thought to attain the highest heaven, because
in the act of killing, Krishna destroys the impurities in their
souls: Krishna kills the lower self. Appropriately, Kashmir,
in northern India, has a reputation of being a refuge for
mystics. Muslim Sufis, Hindu yogis, and Buddhist monks

have all thrived in the beauty of the Kashmiri mountains, valleys, and lakes.

During the days of British India, Kashmir was a principality. It had its own king and administration but was under the sovereign umbrella of the British government. When the British withdrew in 1947, British India was divided into Pakistan and India. Pakistan became an Islamic state established on the theory that Muslims could not get proper representation in India. India remained a secular state (ironically with more Muslims than Pakistan). The many principalities in British India (over five hundred) were forced to join either Pakistan or India. Because Kashmir bordered both Pakistan and India and had a long history and a unique culture, called *Kashmiryat*, that transcended religious ties, it preferred independence. When the British withdrew their sovereign umbrella, Kashmir became legally independent. But political realities made it impossible for them to keep their independence.

Because the majority of people in Kashmir were Muslim, Pakistan insisted that it join Pakistan. India, embracing all faiths, felt that Kashmir should have an equal right to join India but should not remain independent. Pakistan tried to resolve the issue by organizing Pashtoon tribesman to take Kashmir by force. This was an attempt to create an illusion of a people's uprising. Because the tribesmen spent most of their time plundering (instead of taking territory), they were later replaced by regular Pakistani troops. The maharaja of Kashmir appealed to India for protection. India agreed to help on the condition that Kashmir join India, subject to the consent of the Kashmiri people once order was established. Order was never fully established. Kashmir became divided by a "line of control" between the two military forces. Another war was fought, and there have been decades of low-level conflict, placing the Kashmiri people in the cross fire between Indian troops and militant groups supported by Pakistan.

Through UN mediation, India and Pakistan agreed to have a plebiscite to determine the desire of the Kashmiris. But there were problems: the presence of troops created too much influence, it was logistically impossible, and Kashmiris objected to not being given the option of independence. Thus the plebiscite never took place.

WHEN I WAS in New Delhi soliciting help for the Dalai Lama, I also got entangled in the Kashmir dispute. A small nonprofit organization asked me to work with them on Kashmir. The partnership fell apart, but I continued the work on my own and drafted a proposal entitled "Kashmir: A Call for a Constitutional Convention (A Proposal to the People of Kashmir)." Under the Indian constitution, India has sovereign rights over Kashmir in only three areas: international affairs, military, and communication. All other powers were reserved for Kashmir. However, over the decades Kashmir had become directly administered by India, and the Kashmiris resented the loss of their autonomy.

The proposal recommended a constitutional assembly in Kashmir to restore their autonomy. It empowered the Kashmiris by giving them the right to form the assembly on their own. This right, I argued, was protected under Article 370 of the constitution of India. Autonomy, I thought, could bring peace to Kashmir. It would give the Kashmiris the freedom they want, and it would take away the long-standing complaint of Pakistan that India oppresses Kashmir.

The proposal also recommended that the current line of

control be accepted as the international boundary between India and Pakistan. This would be the final act of peace between India and Pakistan. India-controlled Kashmir consists of Ladakh (originally part of Tibet), composed mainly of Buddhists; Jammu, composed mainly of Hindus; and the Valley of Kashmir, composed mainly of Muslims, but culturally unique. Pakistan-controlled Kashmir consists of both Azad (free) Kashmir and the Northern Territories, both composed of Muslims with close cultural ties to Pakistan.

The irony is that the current line of control represents an equitable division of Kashmir. The Hindus and Buddhists clearly prefer India, and the Muslims in the Pakistan-controlled areas clearly prefer Pakistan. The Valley of Kashmir is the real "apple" of dispute and remains the center of military conflict and propaganda wars. The Muslims in this area have generally preferred independence, or at least autonomy, but under a secular India that would respect their unique culture, Kashmiryat.

Kashmiryat is a blend of religion, language, and traditions that forms something unique and distinct from other regions in South Asia. Kashmiryat is strongly influenced by the mysticism of Muslim Sufism, and to some extent by the mysticism of the Hindu yogis and Tibetan Buddhist monks. This undogmatic mystical aspect of Kashmiryat gives it a quality that transcends religious identity. Thus, Kashmiris are not simply Muslim or Hindu, but Kashmiri Muslim or Kashmiri Hindu. But for the people in this beautiful but blood-soaked valley, peace and autonomy remain a dream.

I presented the proposal to Dr. Karan Singh, the crown prince and son to the last maharaja of Kashmir. He never became king because Kashmir became a republic, but he was appointed regent at eighteen and then later became governor. He considered it the first "practical proposal" he had ever read and introduced me to his associates. One of these, Siddik Wahid, was a model Kashmiri: a Muslim from Kashmir's Buddhist area (Ladakh), he practiced Sufi meditation and carried the Bhagavad-Gita, a Hindu scripture, wherever he went. Siddik ensured that the proposal was distributed throughout Kashmir.

I also presented the proposal to Farooq Abdullah, a former chief minister of Kashmir. Farooq did most the talking in our meeting, giving a highly emotional presentation as if speaking to a large crowd. Farooq is a supporter of autonomy and invited me to Shri Nagar, the capital of Kashmir. Farooq's father led the republican political forces against Dr. Singh's father and his monarchy. So the families have never been very close. Recently, however, Forooq became chief minister again and appointed Dr. Karan Singh's son to his cabinet. Time heals.

I gave a copy to Minister Engulf Keisow, a Swedish diplomat I had worked with on the Tibet issue. He surprised me and sent it to the Swedish foreign ministry as a model analysis of the Kashmir issue, telling me that everyone there had read it. I began to think that the proposal had potential.

The big test was the Indian government. I made presentations to the newly formed Indian National Human Rights Commission. The chairman, a friend of Prime Minister Rao, gave Rao a copy of the proposal and it circulated in his cabinet. I never found out any details on the government's response. But I knew that the home minister did not approve of either Kashmiri autonomy or

Americans. Not long afterwards I was asked to leave India. I never made it to Kashmir as I had planned. Perhaps this was a good thing. Shortly after I left India, a militant group in Kashmir took some tourists hostage for ransom. One was beheaded and the others were presumed dead.

When the Rao government left power, the new government of India adopted a policy of autonomy for Kashmir. India floated an offer to Pakistan to accept the line of control as the international boundary. This is exactly what I had pushed for, but Pakistan did not respond the way I had hoped. They rejected the offer, and their policy of supporting militants in Kashmir continues. The continued violence has prevented autonomy from being implemented.

Since 1994, when I was working on this issue, a new breed of militants emerged in Kashmir. Based in Pakistan, often trained in Afghanistan, and with little or no connection to Kashmir, their sole motive is to spread Islamic fundamentalism. This motive obviously conflicts with the undogmatic mysticism that characterizes Kashmiryat, the soul of Kashmir.

As militancy has grown in Kashmir, so has the number of Indian troops to combat militancy. The large numbers of Indian troops attempting to police Kashmir has resulted in extensive human rights abuses. Understandably, the Kashmir people do not think fondly of either India or Pakistan. Any solution to Kashmir must therefore include India's resolve to stop human rights abuses by its soldiers, and Pakistan's resolve to stop the influence of militant fundamentalism in Kashmir.

WHILE I WAS working on the Kashmir issue in New Delhi, the U.S. Assistant Secretary of State, Robin Raphel, visited.

She made some vague statements about Kashmir that led people to believe she was supporting Pakistan's position. I never saw so much anger against a single person. Newspapers were full of political cartoons about her, and even the riksha drivers were making jokes about her.

I know this because I often traveled by "motor riksha," which is a motor scooter with a carriage behind it. They are very maneuverable and drivers weave in and out of traffic, often coming a couple inches from other "vehicles," such as buses, trucks, carts drawn by donkeys, free-walking cows, and an occasional elephant, all ignoring traffic lanes. The cab is open, so the hot polluted air of New Delhi swirls about the passengers. One riksha driver fell asleep and ran off the road, sending the riksha up on its head. He insisted I still pay him for the ride. Another collided with a drunk diplomat, and I had to mediate the affair to keep them from fighting.

Around the time of Raphel's visit, I gave a public lecture on human rights, and a national newspaper covering it referred to me as a former "official" of the U.S. State Department. However, newspapers referred to Robin Raphel as just a "junior official" of the State Department, which I thought was funny. Of course, I was never an official; I just worked there for a bit, whereas Raphel was a senior official.

I was constantly being attacked for U.S. policy, to which I would reply, "It's not me. I'm just a private citizen. It's that silly fellow in the White House." But when I was accused of being a CIA agent or State Department plant (as was sometimes the case), there was no way of countering it, because they always expect you to deny the accusations. All I could say was, "Look how poor I am. Would a CIA agent ride in a riksha?"

PEOPLE IN INDIA often questioned me about why I was involved in these issues. One reason they expected me to be a CIA agent was they figured I must be getting something personal from it. "What's in it for you?" was a typical question. They did not believe me when I said I did this work because I enjoyed it. Because the work was political, they thought "CIA." Many have no concept of "charity" work. In the American legal tradition, charity is called *pro bono publico* (for the good of the public). Here a lawyer works on a case because he wants to see justice done, and for no other reason. I had a passion for this work and was not bothered about living on a low budget and getting nothing in return. In a world run by the ceaseless pursuit of personal desires, this was foreign and unfathomable.

Self-help literature is rich in advice on how to fulfill desires: goal setting, visualizing enjoying your goals, techniques to maintain inspiration and the will to succeed, affirmations to change thought patterns. To the degree that such techniques tear away destructive thinking such as defeatism and depression and replace them with optimism, inspiration, and focus to achieve your dreams, they have a spiritual quality. However, spirituality deals more with the refinement and purification of desire than with the blind pursuit of desires. "Be careful about what you desire because you may get it" is the caveat of the world of desires.

One technique sometimes recommended for acquiring wealth is the practice of charity. The thinking is that if a person gives to charity, that person will receive many-fold in return. This is cited as a law of nature. There may be something there, but what is being returned would not necessarily be money. It could be virtue, contentment, and happiness.

Like the proverbial butterfly that cannot be caught when chased, but alights on the shoulder when you're looking the other way, happiness never comes directly by pursuing selfish ends. It comes indirectly through service to others. In a moral universe, the *intent* of the person is central, not the act. A person who gives money just to get more money is doing business, not charity. In that respect, the giving cannot be called spiritual. However, the act of giving does tend to open the heart, and, whatever the motive, the charitable institution getting the gift receives the benefits all the same.

There is a story about a young yogi in India meditating in the cold foothills of the Himalayas. A rich merchant came up to him and put an expensive shawl around his shoulders. The yogi asked, "Why?" The merchant said, "Because it is said that for any gift given to a saint, one will receive one hundred-fold in return." So the young yogi gave it back to him, saying with a smile, "Here, I'll see what I can do about the other ninety-nine."

The spiritual approach to charity is to give out of love with no thought of reward or recognition. I do not pretend to have mastered this, but I acknowledge it. Nor do I think everyone should do charitable work. It is a personal decision connected to one's interests. Ideally, it should be done because there is a desire to do it, not because of a depressing sense of obligation or a warped view of economics. There also is a practical point: people should not sacrifice themselves as martyrs. One thing I like about the International Red Cross is that they take care of themselves. The staff are well compensated and often well protected.

Much of the growth of the soul involves the refinement of desires, from the coarsest of desires to the most refined.

We either grow out of the coarse desires, or they are burned away by great pain and sorrow. The finer desires emerge by awakening to higher things. The highest desire is the desire to experience God in oneself, to merge the soul into the ocean of bliss.

One person's heaven is another person's hell. For a person of coarse passions, the sight of blood excites, but for the person of refined feelings, the sight of blood nauseates.

In India, as in other places, I often saw the rich and powerful abuse the poor. They look down on them, order them about, and assert an air of superiority. It is very ugly to see. It is a coarse desire to dominate and to feel powerful, and it leads to deep resentment by others. It shuts the heart off, "drying" it out, dragging the soul down a thorny road of unhappiness.

Taking this desire up a few notches, a person begins to feel repelled by this ugliness. Power is exercised by a compassionate mind that treats people with respect and thus earns their respect and admiration. But such a person often becomes attached to the feelings of importance and power, feeling empty upon losing it. The seduction of power is increasingly subtle, which is why politics and the military are such dangerous professions.

A few notches higher on the ladder of desire we find people who exercise power because the silent guide inside them nudged them to exercise power, and because the circumstances of life compelled it. The joy that such people dwell in comes from following the fine impulse of wisdom inside and in the happiness and justice that they help create. Upon losing power, there is no loss of happiness, because the real source of the joy remains: the subtle connection to

God. The attachments are not with the world but with the silent inner voice that guides us through the world.

A painter appreciates color and form at a much higher level than most others. The sight of the painter has become attuned to finer levels of color and texture. The world sparkles and colors are alive. One reason I decided not to continue as an artist was that I knew I could never portray the beauty of the spiritual light I saw. It cannot be painted, and it certainly cannot be sculpted. In the same way, a musician is much more aware of the finer qualities of sound than most of us. Sound is full of life. At more refined levels, I imagine the songs of angels fill the ears of the musician. The blind Irish harpist Turlough O'Carolan is said to have heard the music of faeries. His music, he claimed, was their music put to his harp. The thinker experiences finer levels of thought. Thoughts, like color to the painter or songs to the musician, are full of joy.

Thus in time we all come to appreciate finer and finer levels of life, experiencing higher and more refined levels of joy. The refinement of appreciation directly correlates with the refinement of desire. As our appreciations refine, so do our desires. Eventually, we begin to appreciate the divine joy in the world around us and in the depths of our own being. The spirit of God, emerging as an ocean of bliss, is the culmination of the human quest for higher joys, where the depths of happiness are endless.

NEW DELHI, LIKE many large cities, is a hectic place: huge, sprawled out, polluted, and buzzing with every imaginable human endeavor. So, my days of *pro bono publico* work often ended in exhaustion. Over the years, whenever my days end in such exhaustion and I lie down and close my eyes late at night, my inner light shines brightly and my mind is drawn in to it. The exhaustion is more spiritual than physical. The inner light responds by feeding my soul. I become like a hummingbird at a flower, drinking the nectar of light. My mind kisses the light, merges with it, drinks from it; then a deep sleep falls over me.

Mother Divine

I ARRIVED IN India for my first time in the spring of 1986, a year before I entered law school. As I stepped off the airplane, I was hit by a wave of heat and humidity. But there was also excitement, and my inner light was very bright, pulsating in the night sky. My light often responds this way when I arrive at new places.

The first leg of my journey led me to the ancient town of Ayodhya. Ayodhya is the city where Rama is supposed to have ruled his kingdom in the distant past of India, thousands of years ago. His story is told in the great epic, *Ramayana*. Rama, an incarnation of God, comes to earth to destroy evil, embodied by the demon Ravana. Rama's beautiful wife, Sita, the daughter of the earth, is kidnapped by Ravana. Rama saves her and destroys Ravana with the help of Hanuman, the monkey god.

Hindu religion is famous for its many gods. However, what is often misunderstood is that the many gods are different facets of the one transcendental God, like branches of one great tree. Hindus pray to different gods, depending on their inclination and on what quality of God they wish to invoke. Indian religion is like the Indian culture: rich in variety, yet united at the core.

Hanuman, son of the wind god, had the body of a monkey. In my mind, Hanuman represents the individual human soul that has attained spiritual union with God and draws from God's strength to fulfill the grand design. In India, Hanuman is equated with service to God, and those seeking strength for good projects often pray to Hanuman. I have a friend who worships Hanuman, and he, like Hanuman, is a whirlwind of energy.

Ayodhya is primarily a place of worship. There are Rama and Hanuman temples everywhere. Most notably, there are monkeys everywhere. If you are a monkey, the best place to live is Ayodhya. People respect monkeys there, and tourists often feed them. But the relationship is not altogether friendly. Monkeys are tricky and will snatch things from you, especially food, if you are not looking. Ayodhya is also a place of villages, and I spent some time visiting villages and old ruins. Children would follow me around, first staring wide-eyed as if they were seeing the man from the moon, and then, with the faintest smile from me, bursting into laughter and giggles.

Most of my time in India was spent in the Himalayas. My favorite site was a small village called Gongotri near the source of the river Ganges at an altitude of about 10,000 feet. Gongotri is one of four main pilgrimage destinations in that area and is visited by all sorts of religious tourists and holy people. From Gongotri, I hiked up the river to its source, a glacier in the eternal snows of the Himalayas. I slept that night at a small ashram (monastery). It was so cold that it was difficult to sleep and I had nightmares of being buried alive. The next day, while I was hiking on the glacier, the ice broke from underneath me, and I fell through. I caught myself at the edge of the crevice that had opened up and extended like a wedge about thirty feet below me. I had images of myself falling into the wedge below and becoming an iceman.

Crawling out, I thought that was enough. I hiked back to Gongotri on a trail that hugged the base of large mountains looming up from the river valley. It was spring and the snow was melting, causing rocks to loosen and fall. At one point on the trail I found myself in the middle of falling rocks hurling down from thousands of feet above, creating a whizzing sound as they flew through the air. I hid behind large boulders until there was a pause in the falling rocks, then I ran to the next place of shelter until I got through. Back in Gongotri, I learned that a *sadhu* (holy person) had been killed by falling rocks that day on the same trail. Death teased me twice that day. Such experiences remind us the value of life. I cannot say that I am afraid of death. But I am terrified of the prospect of an early death preventing me from fulfilling my life.

Gongotri was exceptionally beautiful, and I took photos of the temple, river gorges, and such characters as the sadhus, with matted hair and ash-smeared bodies, who spent their life wandering around and singing songs to Shiva. There was a cave built under a large boulder with a small little door attached. It reminded me of a Hobbit's home from J. R. R. Tolkien's mythos. An orange flag flew at the entrance to tell the world that a swami lived there. I was intrigued by it and by the swami. I took a couple of pictures, being careful not to disturb him, and left Gongotri for other adventures.

The Himalayas in this area (between Yamanotri and Badrinath) consisted of villages and assorted pilgrimage sites connected by ancient footpaths and precarious mountain roads. I traveled around by bus, often riding on the top to enjoy the scenery, but having to avoid the low-hanging branches and wires. The best fun were the ancient footpaths meandering through the mountains and valleys. Here I met a goatherd, who invited me to sit with him and have warm goat's milk. His little daughter rolled around laughing with a puppy, while the father and I tried to communicate such simple things as, "I'm from America." Experiences like these filled my days.

I EVENTUALLY SETTLED in a small town called Uttarkashi. There I spent my time writing, meditating, and hiking around the mountains. Falling asleep one day after a meditation, I had a vivid dream of a golden fish that came up from a clear pond and said to me, "Go to Gongotri: you'll find a pot of gold." I was not planning on returning to Gongotri, but such dreams, I have found, usually have something to them.

I have always been fascinated with symbology in dreams, mythology, and art since my teens, when I consumed the works of Carl Jung. I know there are people and cultures that have developed ways of getting guidance from their dreams, but I have never been good at it. I usually forget my dreams. But there are times when my dreams are so vivid that they are imprinted in my memory and cannot be forgotten. These I take notice of. Although symbology is often personal, the symbology of this dream followed classic lines: clear calm water is the spiritual realm, the golden fish is the spiritual messenger, and the pot of gold is spiritual attainment or wisdom. To me, spiritual wisdom is gold. So I returned to Gongotri to see where this might lead.

When I arrived, I asked around about whether there were any respected yogis in town. Two or three people told me about Swami Hansananda, thought to be over one hundred years old. I visited him and found a large man with silver hair and beard, skin that had turned pale with age, and a face that beamed with joy. He told me stories, laughed a lot, and then asked me to go see another swami called Parananda. Swami Parananda, it turned out, was a disciple of his. He was also the swami who lived in that cave under a big rock that I had taken photos of months earlier. He was young for a guru (late thirties), and it turns out that I was the first person his master sent to him to teach.

The contrast between master and disciple was humorous. The master was old, relaxed, unscholarly, and not concerned with tradition. The disciple was young and disciplined, had the mind of a scholar, and was traditional in everything he did. The result was that there was a constant tension between the two, and each would complain to me about the other.

Parananda and I got along the instant we met. He spoke impeccable English, was well read, and knew a number of Hindu scriptures by heart. We would take long walks in the woods or sit next to the Ganges and talk. He would recite scriptures from memory and then comment on them. Or we would talk about spiritual experiences and practices or anything else under the sun. Whenever we were together, a bright white star would appear above us and follow us wherever we went. I was the only person who saw the star. I supposed that it was a projection of my own spiritual sun. I had no idea what it meant except that something good was happening. One day I asked Parananda about it, and he responded with a shrug, saying, "I don't know everything." He was an honest swami.

Parananda once offered to teach me some "powers." I consider the highest power to be grace. Grace is that magic around a person that comes from being close to God. It lights our way. It is a silent power that protects and guides us through the storms of life. I told this to Parananda, who seemed amused by my reasoning and rejection of his offer. If I learned such powers (a very big "if"), it would probably just get me into trouble.

I'm not sure what powers Parananda had in mind, but he would exercise them on occasion. He once (clairvoyantly) watched me with his inner eye to see how I was doing during my meditations and later reprimanded me for swaying my body back and forth. I always meditated alone in a small room far away from his cave.

Another time he projected himself to me, appearing in my inner eye during meditation, and spoke. When I met him afterwards, he repeated what he had said to me during meditation. Apparently this can also be done in dreams. Parananda told a story of a yogi who once requested some free goods from a merchant. When the merchant refused him, the yogi visited the merchant in his dreams and threatened him. The yogi got his goods. I asked Parananda, "Why would a yogi do such an unspiritual thing as bully someone in their dreams?" Throwing his hands up in the air, he responded, "Who says yogis are enlightened?"

There is a saying in India that the first guru is the parent, the second is the spiritual teacher, and the third and last is the Self. The real guru is the Self, because our direct connection to God is there. I have never had a guru in the traditional sense, but I try to learn from people when I can. Parananda knew a lot about an ancient practice called *Shri Vidya* (knowledge of Mother Divine), which he had learned in Kashmir.

In Shri Vidya, Mother Divine is perceived as that aspect of God that is active, creative, and nurturing. And Shiva is perceived as that aspect of God that is nonactive and eternal. In the practice of *Shri Vidya*, Mother Divine transforms the soul and body to prepare it to house the eternal spirit, Shiva. When this is attained, it is said that Mother Divine and Shiva have "married" inside the person. This, of course, is an allegorical description of spiritual transformation.

Initiating me into this practice, Parananda had me do long hours of *japa* on a mantra (a name or attribute of God) of Mother Divine. In japa, one uses a string of beads called a mala. With one hand, you move from bead to bead, going through the whole string of one hundred and eight beads, and then repeat the process. With each bead, you repeat a mantra. Going from bead to bead reciting a mantra allows the mind to keep focused; it also is a way to keep track of how many times the mantra is repeated. Its purpose is to generate spiritual energy and unleash a transformation. It is a universal practice, common among Hindus, Buddhists, Muslims, and Catholics. Hours of this practice each day was not easy, and I complained, getting only a frown in response. Parananda did things in accord with tradition, and there was no getting around this.

One day, after a couple of weeks of practice, I experienced the fruit of my efforts. During meditation, I became aware of a blue light. It got brighter, until I found myself immersed in a sea of blue light. It was the light of consciousness, the life and being of pure beauty. It reminded me of the realm of absolute beauty described in Plato's *Symposium*. It was as if the concentration of all the beauty in life was present in it. After my soul had drunk its fill from this sea of beauty, I was pulled out. All I could think was "How beautiful! How so very beautiful!"

The blue light continued to flicker about me. It has never left me and remains like a small blue star, sometimes growing big, sometimes hardly noticeable, shining in and around the pool of white light in my soul.

When I asked Parananda what this blue light was, he said without a pause, "Mother Divine." I have a friend who also experienced a spiritual blue light but refers to it as the light of Christ. Seeing the light in terms of Christ or Mother Divine is a matter of preference. Both are true. Spiritual reality is far beyond our religious or spiritual frameworks. But what is clear to me is that the blue light is a spectrum of divine being. It is a quality of pure spirit made manifest.

IMMANUEL KANT ARGUED that the human mind is like a pair of glasses that color our perception of the world. Kant argued that the human mind can thus never penetrate into the real essence of things. But he also argued that the fact that humans have some success in the world reveals that there must be some correlation between human reason and reality. Most physical scientists tend to agree with Kant and narrow their notion of reality to time, space, and abstract forces. Taste, color, sound, texture, beauty, emotions, and love are all human projections and are the subject of the arts, philosophy, and such "soft sciences" as psychology.

However, if we imagine that humans were, as Genesis proclaims, made in the image of God, then human minds are faint images of the mind of God. Human intelligence is, despite its fallibility, fashioned along the lines of a much higher intelligence. Thus taste, color, sound, and especially love and beauty reflect this higher intelligence. They are inklings of a higher mind, a faint shimmering reflection of a great sun. In its spiritual quest, the soul grows to reflect the sun fully as a polished mirror and then merges with it, becoming the light it once knew only as a faint reflection. Thus the soul penetrates into the essence of life.

For much of the twentieth century, physics has been striving for a unified theory of the forces of nature. Stephen Hawking, in *A Brief History of Time*, speculates that when this is achieved, humanity may have a glimpse into the mind of God. I think Hawking would agree that because physics deals mainly with mathematical models of nature, we will only be glimpsing the mathematician in God. I think he would also agree that the author, artist, and musician in God are equally important.

But if there is anything fundamental to reality, it would not be mathematics but love and beauty that permeate and give life its meaning and substance. The reality beyond the images of life is not a web of blind physical forces but the love of a divine artist. The universe was not created from the violence of a big bang but emerged from the harmonies of a grand symphony. The highest truth of life is its incredible beauty. We can analyze a sunrise in terms of the refraction of light through the atmosphere and its effect on the retina of the eye. But the experience of its beauty—the red and orange hues spreading out in a blue sky—is much closer to reality. Truth is not a set of propositions in a textbook but a state of being infused with vast beauty.

There is a line from *The Prophet* by Kahlil Gibran that says, "Beauty is life when life unveils her holy face." Gibran adds, "But you are life and you are the veil." For most of us the veil is lifted ever so slowly by the refinement of our desires and perceptions. As humanity rises to higher appreciations of beauty, our desires begin to harmonize and peace dawns in the world.

PARANANDA TOLD ME that there is a legend that Mother Divine has her earthly seat in Kashmir at a place called Keer Bhavan. This is a small pool that changes color to predict the coming year. Before World War II, it was reported to have been blood red. Kashmir is known for beauty, the essence of Mother Divine. Because of its beauty and because of its history as a sanctuary for mystics, many people look at Kashmir as a battleground between light and darkness, spirituality and materiality. Many devotees believe that Mother Divine will dawn all over the world, spreading her sovereign "cloak" to establish a new era of peace.

Once during meditation, I experienced a darkness entering me and smothering me. It got stronger and stronger, and at the point where I felt like being drowned and extinguished by it, there was an explosion of white light and the darkness was gone. There is something universal about this experience. Life can take only so much darkness until there is a violent reaction against it. Kashmir can absorb only so much darkness until something snaps and a transformation becomes inevitable.

In the spring of 1998, India and Pakistan came close to war over Kashmir, this time sparked by the testing of nuclear arms. And in the summer of 1999, India and Pakistan clashed at Kargil, northern Kashmir. It was the first time in history that two nuclear powers fought directly against each other. Nuclear war hangs over Kashmir like a ghost, reminding them of the necessity for reconciliation.

The challenge of a mediator is to redirect the forces of conflict so that transformation comes about through peaceful means, not through war. But the power of a mediator is highly limited. The mediator can only facilitate reconciliation, helping it along like a midwife. If the potential for peace does not exist within the people, little can be done.

In the story of the *Mahabharata*, Lord Krishna attempted to mediate a peaceful settlement between ruling cousins at the brink of war. All the kings of the world, the story goes, were assembled behind them. But even Lord Krishna, the incarnation of God, was not successful in instilling rationality into the storm of passions. The earth had absorbed so much negativity, only the violent storms of war could wash it away.

When I was involved in this issue, I had a vision of standing in the Kashmir valley. Kashmir was free, and peace and love filled the valley. Kashmir, like much of the world, is pregnant with this ideal. And it is pushing itself out against a resisting world.

4

BURMA

Disciple: Tell me about woman.

*Master: Mystery, creative power, beauty, source
of life, love. It is said that woman
brought man down from the trees and
she'll probably bring him into a new
age.*

A Stop in Rangoon

BURMA (NOW OFFICIALLY named Myanmar) came into my
life by accident. In Kathmandu and Beijing I tried to get
an Indian visa but was rejected. I was on their notorious
"blacklist" because of my work in Kashmir. A tourist in
Beijing who had been in Burma told me that an Indian
visa could be obtained in Burma in one day. This meant
the embassy did not have the time to check with Delhi and
the blacklist. To get back into India, I decided to be tricky
and get my visa in Burma.

A trip to Burma meant first going to Bangkok, the
travel hub of Southeast Asia. Like Kathmandu, Bangkok is
geared for the tourist. One of its largest industries is

prostitution. Pamphlets are distributed much like any other tourist attraction, with pictures of smiling women and staff, all in uniforms. While walking out of a restaurant one day, I met a young woman about seventeen years old who was standing next to the register. In her white translucent dress, she looked like a little China doll. I asked her if she worked there or was related to the owner. She smiled and said "yes." She did not understand my questions; she was just smiling and saying "yes." I realized she was soliciting business. I doubt she had long to wait.

Prostitution is a difficult issue. It is clearly not something I would recommend to anyone for a livelihood. Trading sex for money takes sex out of the realm of love and puts it into the realm of greed and lust. It is an abuse of sexual energy. However, for many it may be the only form of affection they will know.

Generally, it is never easy to judge the behavior of others, especially in consensual relations between two adults where there is no victim. But the big problem in prostitution is not whether a woman freely chooses prostitution over other professions or whether a man chooses it as a way of relieving sexual tension or for companionship. The problem is in the extremes of lust and greed that result in forced prostitution and child prostitution through economic, emotional, and physical coercion. These practices do serious damage to fragile souls.

Every woman, I would like to think, is a blossoming Mother Divine, a soul awakening to its own divinity. Like flowers, they should not be trampled on. I read an account of a Thai family that forced their daughter into prostitution so they could afford to buy a TV and VCR. This type of thinking is a growing "cancer" in Thailand

and much of the world. There is no simple answer. Like all social problems, prostitution is ultimately a spiritual problem, because it is rooted in the evolution of the soul of society. In a society permeated with love, I doubt that prostitution would ever be a consideration.

WOMEN TEND TO be a great mystery to most men. Men tend to be locked on a mental-physical level, whereas women, closer to their feelings and intuition, have a more transcendental quality to them. The fact that a woman is physically involved in conceiving, nurturing, and giving birth to a new human being makes her a real part of the creative forces of nature. Considering this role, it is easy to understand why women would have a higher emotional and intuitive quality: childbirth puts them in touch with this creative process and with the forces of nature. Men, by contrast, are merely catalysts (biologically speaking), far removed from nature's raw creative powers.

Most cultures have noticed that the differences seen in the sexes are also seen in nature. The Chinese describe this as the doctrine of yin and yang: feminine and masculine qualities permeating life. Some argue that this is mere anthropomorphism, projecting human qualities onto natural phenomena. But I am convinced it is more an acknowledgment of similarities between the sexes and nature.

Masculine energy is electric and centrifugal, while feminine energy is magnetic and centripetal (like a whirlpool). This is seen in personality traits and sexual energy. Women are beautiful and attract; men are aggressive and pursue. Men are easily aroused and quick to ground out, like bolts of electricity; women are slower to arouse and slower to fulfill, making them sexually superior. Men tend to approach women from the level of passion; women approach men from the level of love. Men are forced to rise to the level of love, usually (from a woman's point of view) through a long frustrating process. This is an oversimplification, of course, but I think there is some truth there.

Early humans saw the sun and rain warm and drench the earth; then they saw the earth give birth to its fruit. Then they saw men giving warmth and raining semen inside women, and women giving birth. Thus they saw a clear analogy, a universal principle. Women are like earth; earth is like women. It makes sense that because we are the fruit of nature, we would also exhibit qualities found in nature. A man and a woman together create a wholeness, reflecting the wholeness of nature.

According to the doctrine of reincarnation, the human soul is neither male nor female, but encompasses both qualities. A central principle of reincarnation is balanced growth: the soul goes through various experiences to awaken all spiritual qualities and to achieve completeness. If a soul remained only with one sex, it would become lopsided and unbalanced. After a few incarnations as a male, the soul is forced to begin incarnations as a female to maintain spiritual balance, to develop feminine qualities that it has neglected.

Most men, including myself, upon having a dream of being a woman, would consider it a nightmare and wake up in a cold sweat, thanking God it was only a dream. But on the other side, where the soul is infused with a higher wisdom, it understands the necessity of moving on to other things. A soul can learn only so much by being a John Wayne or a Winston Churchill. So when it reaches the outer boundaries of a particular gender, it bounces back to the other side.

In India it is believed that homosexuality and bisexuality are a result of the crossover by the soul from one gender to the other. Thus a manly woman or a feminine man are considered recent crossovers. It is a common saying by homosexuals that they feel like a woman trapped in a man's body or a man trapped in a woman's body. This leads some men to joke that they are lesbians trapped in a man's body. Occasionally, a soul remains attached to past sexual and romantic tendencies after a crossover, and thus tends toward homosexuality and bisexuality. There may be other reasons for homosexuality, but this is a central factor cited under the doctrine of reincarnation.

This principle of balance applies to other aspects of the soul as well. A soul spending lifetimes as an athlete or policeman to develop willpower and inner strength may, out of necessity, return to develop caring qualities as a physician or monk. A scientist or scholar spending lifetimes sharpening the mind may feel compelled to live a life as a painter, musician, or craftsman to unfold the more subtle aspects of perception and to balance a highly developed intellect. No quality of the soul is left dormant; every facet is to be awakened, polished, and brought out to its highest spiritual gloss.

The principle of balance applies to society as well. Female political leaders are common in Asia. Often, as spouses or daughters of slain leaders, they have arisen in Burma, the Philippines, Sri Lanka, India, Pakistan, Indonesia, and Bangladesh. Ruled for so long by governments dominated by corrupt men, it is as if these people are seeking balance in their governments in the hopes of restoring justice in society. It is common in daily life that when men lose themselves in the material world, women are often there to remind them of the spiritual world, restoring a balance.

IN BURMA, THE rising star of democracy is Lady Aung San Suu Kyi. Suu Kyi has been challenging the harsh practices of the Burmese military regime for a decade. She leads the forces in the Burmese society that seek balance through the promotion of democracy and human rights.

Burma is primarily a Buddhist nation, though it has borrowed some customs from its Hindu neighbors in India, including the idea of "divine kingship" that prevailed in Burma as the political system during Asia's feudal era. After three wars with the British in the nineteenth century, Burma became a British colony. Like India, Burma got its independence from Britain after World War II. General Aung San (Suu Kyi's father) was a political leader in the independence movement but was assassinated while he was forming the first civil government. Despite the assassination, a civil government was formed, which lasted until 1962, when the military took over.

The military regime promoted a socialist system that destroyed the economy. In 1987 the regime finally conceded that the socialist formula did not work. After much civil unrest, elections were held in 1990. Suu Kyi won the election by a overwhelming majority, but the military regime did not have the strength to transfer power. A standoff continues between the forces of democracy led by Suu Kyi and the outdated military regime.

I spent about one week in Rangoon, Burma's capital, getting the visa for India. As usual, I was on a low-income budget and found cheap lodging at the local YMCA. The first thing that struck me was the traditional dress of the men. They all wore lungis, a long cloth wrapped around the waist, forming a dress. You also see this in India, mainly in Bengal and the South. I bought a green plaid one of a cotton and silk mix to wear around town. Women, to keep cool and fragrant, put sandalwood paste on their cheeks and foreheads and flowers in their hair.

I befriended some lawyers, who introduced me to the world of Rangoon. The legal system, borrowed from the British, is highly developed. However, it is limited to civil and commercial disputes. Citizens cannot challenge the government on political matters. The best way to understand the political environment of a country is to be there and talk to as many people as possible. I spent many hours sitting on six-inch-high stools around a foot-high table, listening to stories and sipping green tea.

At a tea stall near the university, I heard accounts of the crackdown on the students in 1988. It is believed that about four thousand people were killed during this time, many of them students, and that ten thousand students fled to the border. In terms of human life, it was a far greater tragedy than China's Tiananmen Square, where a few hundred people were killed, mostly nonstudents who challenged the military on the roads leading to the square. Not many know about the student massacre in Burma. For the Burmese, it remains a deep scar in their memory.

When people mentioned the student crackdown to me, their voices changed and rage and hurt flickered in their eyes. The gory tales I will leave untold here. But one story I found very amusing was told by a friend who was a student at the time: "During this time, soldiers automatically considered you a student if you wore glasses. I threw my glasses away as I was running to escape the soldiers. I was so afraid that when I threw them away, my eyes became normal and I could see! I still don't have to wear glasses." I believed him.

The people have established an unwritten understanding with the military regime. As long as they do not interfere with the government, they can freely pursue their private lives. Those who get too political may be visited at night and taken to jail. Walking around Rangoon, I felt no indication of this repression. The people are very friendly and generally happy in the bustle of daily living. That does not mean repression was not there; it was just hidden in the shadows.

The only obvious signs of the regime, besides occasional soldiers on the street, are the state-controlled newspaper, radio, and TV. Most news comes from radio through the Voice of America and the BBC and through international magazines, like *Time*, that trickle into the market. Word-of-mouth is another effective source of information. There is a vast network that leaks information into the private sector through contacts in government. This is how I got my information.

AUNG SAN SUU Kyi has become an icon of democracy. For many Burmese she is an angel, pointing her finger toward a future of harmony and prosperity. Most Burmese consider it a truism that Suu Kyi will eventually assume leadership, that it has already been fated and is just a matter of time. What most people do not realize is that the organization under her does not enjoy the same support. As one Burmese told me, "They just want power." Like the Tibet-China issue, the media has oversimplified the conflict. It is not black and white. But clearly Suu Kyi herself is a champion of democracy and human rights and enjoys wide support.

When I arrived in the summer of 1995, she was still under house arrest for, essentially, winning the election in 1990. The popular response of the West has been to demonize the military regime. A more practical approach would be to attempt to see where they are coming from, not to justify but to understand them. They believe that a strong military regime is necessary to bring the country through turbulent times. They consider themselves a "transitional" government acting as a guardian until, in their judgment, a transition to a civil government is possible. Self-interest explains much of their actions. But mainly, I think, it is fear and lack of experience in democracy.

Suu Kyi's basic policy is reconciliation through dialogue. Like the Dalai Lama, she rejects the use of violence, and, like him, she has been awarded the Nobel Peace Prize for this. However, she continues to support economic sanctions. In fact, she has warned companies that if they invest in Burma, she will remember this when she comes to power. The idea is to bring the government to its knees and force a change. The economy is already weak after decades of a policy of economic isolation. Although the military regime has been trying to open the economy up with well-crafted investment laws and incentives, the economy barely squeaks by. U.S. economic sanctions have not helped matters.

Economic sanctions are best used in specific categories such as prohibiting the import of goods produced by child labor or in prohibiting international loans and grants to regimes that will not use the money for the welfare of the people. Broad economic sanctions are indiscriminate and hurt everyone.

The arm of poverty reaches far, and its touch is harsh, especially on children and the poor. In this regard, broad economic sanctions are a form of indiscriminate violence. To give a small example of this, young Burmese women go to Thailand on promises of work in hotels and restaurants, with hopes of bringing money home. As illegal aliens without visas, they are at the mercy of the Thais, who solicit them and force them into prostitution. Unable to protect themselves, they contract HIV and then, used and abused, are sent back to Burma. At home, they are rejected and face a life of humiliation and slow death. Such tragedies, rather than democratic change, are more often the result of economic sanctions.

The alternative principle of "constructive engagement," coupled by specific sanctions, as used by the United States with China, helps everyone, including the forces of democracy. The best thing for democracy is a growing educated middle class that moves into business and the government, transforming the country. With a growing economy comes greater integration with the global village and vibrant political change.

With my new Indian visa, I left Burma for India on the Bangladesh airlines. As I was in line at immigration in Calcutta, I noticed they were using a computer, and thought, "Oh-oh, I'm in big trouble." As feared, my name popped up with the sentence: "Not to enter India." They had to deport me, but they were gentlemen in doing it. The problem was the airline. They insisted that I pay the return fare. Apparently, they have been able to intimidate most people into doing this. But I knew I was not obligated to pay for my own deportation. Besides, I had little money at the time. In fact, a Polish fellow I flew in with from Rangoon, after seeing me dragged away, pushed twenty dollars into my hand, saying, "You'll probably need this more than I." He was insightful. The Indians finally forced the airline to take me back. I went only as far as Dhaka, Bangladesh, where the airline kept me for a few hours until I finally wore them down and they returned my passport.

From Dhaka, I took a bus to the north in search for the smallest Bangladesh-India border post I could find. I wanted to make sure there was no computer or even a list that would have my name on it. Bangladesh is a land of rivers and water. The bus had to ferry across one river—the Brahmaputra, I guess—that looked like the ocean.

I found one border post so small it was closed. I had gone too far north. The next alternative was a place called Dinajpur, about seventy miles southeast of Nepal. It was small enough, but it was not easy getting through. The immigration officer was very suspicious and asked me numerous questions about the O. J. Simpson case. I cared little for the case and was so exhausted from the trip and the oppressive heat that I gave him very unsatisfactory answers. The customs officer found my old passport in my baggage that had evidence of me being expelled from India. He studied it for a few minutes and then asked, "But where's the visa?" That was a relief. I gave him the new passport and got through, but only after I gave some "presents" to the guy who stamped my visa (a lighter and yellow Post-It notes).

By bus and train I made my way to Saranath, near Varanasi, India. Buses and trains are very different in this part of the world. The bus from Dinjapur had wooden seats and looked like it was fifty years old. Most of the passengers were farmers, some carrying chickens or goats. But the people were invariably friendly.

With an "unreserved" ticket for the train, I was put in a packed compartment, where I stood most of the journey. The conductor tried to blackmail more money from passengers on threat of kicking them out and tried this on me. I was so tired and irritable, I just yelled at him and he left me alone. On the train I met a small boy about ten years old who was traveling and living by himself. We talked with our eyes and hands. And I watched in admiration as he defended his place in the train against an old man. He was remarkably free, independent, and strong-willed. He was a street kid, his only teacher being himself and the life around him.

When I reached Sarnath, I went to the Institute of Higher Tibetan Studies, where I was accepted as a guest of Samdhong Rinpoche. It was a publicly funded institute, but the Rinpoche was responsible for developing it and was the director. The next day, as I was walking through the campus, a great peace and spiritual presence descended on me. Stress and anxiety from months of travel vanished. My mind became perfectly silent and the light from my spiritual sun shone brightly, pulsating around me. There was no desire or anticipation, just a profound, vast peace. This lasted a couple of days and then lingered like the feeling you get after listening to a pleasant tune. It was almost symbolic. Lord Buddha gave his first sermon there at a place in Sarnath called Deer Park. A student from the institute took me there and we fed the deer.

Return to Rangoon

MONTHS LATER, BEFORE leaving for the United States, I contacted my friends in Burma. Suu Kyi had been released from house arrest, and my friends promised to arrange a meeting for me with her. It was January of 1996 when I arrived, but it was still hot in Rangoon. My friend Peter Gold, an anthropologist, was also there recording Burmese folk music, and we visited the Shwe Dagon Pagoda, a huge Buddhist temple on a hill in the middle of the city.

A Burmese friend considers me a Buddhist because I practice meditation and visit temples. My response to her was that I respect all traditions, including Buddhism. But for her, if I seek nirvana through meditation, I am a Buddhist. One day in meditation an image of a Burmese currency note with a picture of Suu Kyi appeared before my inner eye. I mentioned this to my friend, and she took it as a omen of good things to come.

My appointment with Suu Kyi was set when I arrived. But then it was postponed and eventually canceled because tensions began to rise between Suu Kyi's organization and the military regime. Some time earlier, Suu Kyi had withdrawn her party members from the constitutional assembly. Once a constitution is drafted and ratified, a new government is supposed to be formed. But the assembly had been going on for years with no result. Suu Kyi was protesting against this fact, but the regime took it too personally.

Members of her organization told me that the political situation was bad. "It's very, very serious, do you understand?" They spoke with trembling fear. Having seen death and violence in their streets and having friends in jail, the approaching shadow was very real to them. I mentioned this to the political counselor at the U.S. embassy in Rangoon, but he brushed it aside. Some time after I left, mass arrests occurred, but the people were eventually released. The regime just wanted to show everyone who the boss was.

My Burmese friends told me that much of the conflict stemmed from a visit a few months earlier from the (then) U.S. ambassador to the UN, Madeline Albright. They told me that Albright "talked down" to the generals and encouraged Suu Kyi to take a tougher stand. I told my friends that Albright was a great spokeswoman and did not lack in bellicosity but was not a mediator. She just stirred the hornet's nest.

I ADMIT TO "judging" Albright and may be wrong. I am always willing to readjust my judgment by further reflection and experience. "Do not judge others" is a common directive we give to each other. But it cannot be taken literally. If we did not judge others, we could not live. We could not vote or discuss politics, do business, date, or have meaningful relations of any kind. I certainly would not be able to do any mediation where I need to assess the sincerity and motives of people.

The saying "do not judge" has a more subtle meaning. It points to the need for open-mindedness and clarity. It is clearly a warning against the sometimes unnoticeable influences of prejudices rooted deep in our minds. It is also a warning against hasty judgments and judgments warped by our own fears, desires, and anxieties. And it is certainly a warning against clinging to our judgments and not being open to changing them. In essence, "not to judge" means "to judge," but with an open and compassionate mind, keenly aware of one's limitations in perception and wisdom.

Judging is often associated with faultfinding. But many people err in the other direction by imposing good intentions where they do not exist. In a violent world, being too trustworthy is highly dangerous. We have to be "on our toes" for this type of misjudgment as well.

Some people attempt to take the advice of "not judging" literally and do their best to avoid or suspend judgment. This is impossible and sometimes dangerous, and it has the effect of preventing these people from developing the art of judging. One simple practice people can engage in is to judge when it is necessary and to suspend judgment when it is not. If we were honest with ourselves, we would suspend much of our judgment, because our ability to see within the souls of others is so limited.

Again, the emphasis should not be on judging or not judging, but in the refinement and art of judging. We must learn to be receptive to what is around us instead of projecting our fears, prejudices, and anxieties onto the world. There was a young African-American woman in law school who was sensitive about the issue of racial discrimination. I mentioned to her that there is "bad discrimination and good discrimination." "What's good discrimination?" she asked with suspicion. I lifted up my arms and said, "You're so-o-o beautiful!" She smiled and walked away.

On the one extreme of judging there is faultfinding, gossip, and the vast spectrum of prejudice. On the other is the clear heart that sees God in all things, the heart that touches the divine in the hearts of others. That is one big contrast.

The execution of Socrates, the crucifixion of Christ, the Catholic inquisition, and the Holocaust are historical landmarks of warped human judgment. Christ was judged and sentenced by the Jewish priesthood (council of rabbis). Even though they were trained in religious matters, they saw Christ narrowly as a threat to their authority. If they had set their fears aside and listened closely, they may have felt something extraordinarily profound in the man. The crucifixion of Christ came to symbolize the worst form of judging: projecting the "mud" in our minds onto God.

To some extent, we are all guilty of the great sin of the crucifixion. We are continually "crucifying" others and life in general on the "cross" of our own prejudices and relatively dull minds. The process of growing out of this, of perceiving progressively greater levels of beauty in life, of realizing progressively higher levels of love and peace inside us, is central to the path of peace the world is set on.

ABSENT A FORMAL meeting, my Burmese friends asked me to put my ideas in writing so they could present them to Suu Kyi. Generally, mediation involves a lot of personal interaction. People first have to get to know you and you have to get to know them. Then something can happen. A letter from a stranger has little effect. However, a letter presented through interested Burmese would at least warrant serious consideration. Most important, it would provide a way for the Burmese to become directly engaged in the dialogue with the military regime and with Suu Kyi's democracy movement. It would provide a platform for internal dialogue. So I drafted the letter, and it was presented after I left. I planted the seeds, not knowing their effect.

My assessment was this: Suu Kyi is such a powerful rallying point for the Burmese that no matter what she does, she will eventually be successful in bringing democracy to Burma. However, her policy decisions in bringing about this change may speed or slow things up, may promote peaceful transition or violent transition. Her current policies, such as withdrawal from the constitutional assembly and economic sanctions, have only alienated the military regime.

Although the regime has offered to talk to her representatives, she has rejected them, insisting on direct talks. A better policy for her would have been to engage in indirect talks and to get behind the regime on basic issues, such as economic development, while still promoting human rights and democracy. Indirect talks always precede direct talks, especially in emotionally charged disputes.

In the letter I recommended that her party unconditionally return to the constitutional convention. This would restore an atmosphere conducive to talks. I also recommended that they should explore a transitional form of government involving power sharing with the military. One possibility was to allow the military to appoint one-third of the upper house of parliament and one-third of the executive cabinet. This would ensure that the military's interests were protected, while allowing for a transition to civilian rule.

"A special concern," I wrote, "to make the sharing of power possible, is a strong provision giving amnesty to official acts during the period of military rule. However, a claims commission could eventually be set up by legislation to give compensation for damages and injuries during this time, without making criminal charges." Regimes find it difficult to surrender power when they think they may be jailed by the next government. Thus amnesty provisions are common among transitions from oppressive regimes to democratic ones. However, there still remains the need for healing and justice. South Africa and El Salvador addressed this need with "truth commissions" that had the power to investigate human rights violations by the governments and the insurgents but not to prosecute. The underlying philosophy is that truth alone has the power to heal and allow the country to move forward.

This was my opinion as a onlooker. In the end, it may prove to be hogwash. But it does represent the ideal approach, an approach that minimizes violence and brings about change by evolutionary steps. Suu Kyi is in the hot seat, under pressure that is beyond my comprehension. In this respect, she is in the best position to judge what is best. However, she may be too close to the action, and her perception may be clouded by the whirlwind around her. The mediator, being uninvolved, makes suggestions not influenced by the passions of the conflict.

Some of my Burmese friends would say in frustration, "If only the United States would invade Burma as they did Panama and Haiti. Then we would have peace." "That will never happen," I told them, and added, "You just have to evolve out of it."

ODDLY, I SOMETIMES find myself advocating violence as a means for change. I think military intervention was the only answer in Bosnia and Kosovo. When I read about the famine in Sudan in the summer of 1998 caused by their civil war, I immediately thought of a strong military intervention as a solution. Clearly, intervention is a solution of last resort, plagued by political and military nightmares. It is a difficult decision to make as a policymaker, but one that must be faced. In our interdependent world, the decision *not* to intervene may have graver consequences than the decision to intervene.

When I was at "L" at the State Department, we got a new head of the department called "the legal adviser." He was very democratic in his approach and invited everyone to write him a memo with any comments or suggestions they might have. So even though I was just a peon, I was able to contribute my thoughts on issues I was concerned with.

At the end of the Gulf War in 1991, Saddam reasserted his power over Iraq by violently repressing his people, especially the Kurdish minorities in the North. "L" was involved in the drafting of a UN Security Council resolution authorizing the allied forces to intervene to protect them. The UN Security Council, under Chapter 7 of the UN Charter, may authorize the use of military force against a nation if they find the nation's actions to be a "threat to international peace and security."

"L" lawyers wanted the resolution to read that Saddam's actions were a threat to international peace because of the massive flow of refugees over the borders. Their thinking was to narrow the scope of this power to events occurring over national boundaries and not to events within the borders of a nation. However, other lawyers involved wanted the resolution to read that there was a threat to international peace created solely by Saddam's repression of his own people, without respect to national borders. The end result was that the resolution said both, coming across as a little vague. Arguments over the language of legal documents, including such seemingly small matters as a comma, make up the life of lawyers.

I complained to the legal adviser that "L's" contribution was opposed to the development of international law. This development, especially after World War II, brought the actions of governments against their own people under international scrutiny through the vast array of human rights laws. What is "international," and the concern of the international community, and what is "domestic," and the sole concern of a nation, are evolving concepts. "International" no longer means what happens across borders, but what happens *within* borders as well. "L" lawyers knew this but were cautious of extending the power of the UN Security Council. But genocide, massive repression, and other "crimes against humanity" are actions that governments should not feel comfortable engaging in within the protective walls of their national borders.

The new legal adviser at the "L" was an African-American with experience in civil rights law. So he found it easy to agree with me and assure me that, in the future, "L" would give the resolution the liberal interpretation that violent repression of minorities constituted a threat to international peace and security.

A few years later, after I had left "L," the United States found itself intervening again to protect the Kurds in Iraq, who were being repressed but who were not fleeing over the borders. The State Department justified its actions on the earlier UN resolution, using just this interpretation. I eagerly wrote an op-ed for the *Washington Times* explaining the legal interpretation.

The right of one nation to militarily intervene in another nation to protect people against atrocities committed by their own government is actually an old doctrine called "humanitarian intervention." Hugo Grotius, the Dutch father of international law, traces the doctrine back into the mists of antiquity. In the early 1600s, Grotius argued that sovereignty and national borders do not cut off the bonds of humanity that bind us together as one global family. Certain actions by a government against its own people are so atrocious and shocking that there is a moral right and even an obligation to intervene. This human connection prevents us from standing by and doing nothing.

As a legal doctrine, humanitarian intervention has often been under attack because of its reputation of being abused as a pretext for conquest. China, for example, helped to justify its conquest of Tibet as an intervention to rid Tibet from the abuses of feudalism. Some legal scholars assert that the UN Charter supersedes this doctrine, that only the UN may authorize humanitarian intervention. I disagree. As is often the case, there are legal arguments that can be made for and against this position. But from a practical consideration, the UN is often too slow and incompetent for effective action. Further, the doctrine of humanitarian intervention remains deeply rooted in our moral nature, and like the right to self-defense, seems to be inherent in our nature as humans. It cannot be easily written away by legal construction. The doctrine is more rooted in morality than law, and thus in the case of Kosovo in 1999, the United States spoke of a "moral imperative" to justify intervention instead of invoking a point of law. The case of Kosovo, however, also reveals how messy intervention is in actual application and why it is seen as a last resort.

THE BURMESE MILITARY regime is not going anywhere. It has to be dealt with. The real challenge is to transform fear and alienation to trust and cooperation. The transformation of negative energy to positive energy—of anger to love, of suspicion to trust—is the most fundamental principle in spiritual and social change. Like the Tibetans, this is the challenge facing Aung Sang Suu Kyi.

5

AFGHANISTAN

*Disciple: Why is there war in a universe ruled
by a spirit of love?*

*Master: War is a clash of coarse passions that
seek their own death. In time the lower
passions are burned away, love dawns,
and peace reigns, inshallah (God
willing).*

Road to Kabul

AFGHANISTAN IS THE crossroads of Asia. For ages,
merchants and armies passed through Afghanistan,
creating a colorful but often violent history. Alexander the
Great, Genghis Khan, the British, and the Soviets all left
their mark. During the Cold War, the United States and
the USSR competed for influence in Afghanistan through
their aid programs. I met a number of older Afghans who
told me of the "golden" years, when Afghanistan was full
of American teachers, engineers, and agriculturists. It was
golden because it was relatively peaceful and prosperous.

Soviet influence led to the rise of a communist government in Afghanistan, whose policies soon became resented by the people. When the government was on the verge of collapse in 1979, the Soviets invaded Afghanistan to prop it up, thus beginning ten years of *jihad* (holy war) between the *mujahadeen* (holy warriors) and the Soviets.

When the Soviets withdrew in 1989, they left one million Afghans dead and five million as refugees in neighboring countries. The countryside was littered with relics of war and millions of land mines. With the Soviets gone, Afghans began fighting each other, causing tens of thousands more deaths and plunging the country into severe poverty. As of this writing, civil war is still raging between the fundamentalist Taliban in the South and the Northern Alliance.

While visiting Washington, D.C., an Afghan friend of mine from law school told me he thought I should apply my experience as a mediator to the Afghanistan problem. He arranged a meeting for me with Ambassador Mohabhat (representing the Northern Alliance). This led to a formal invitation for me to provide my "services as an independent mediator among the warring parties of Afghanistan." Not long afterwards, the Taliban delegation came through Washington. The head of the delegation, Wakhil Ahmad, wrote me a letter of invitation by hand on my own legal pad, referring to me not by name but simply as "this American." But that was sufficient. Wakhil Ahmad was spokesperson and a type of chief of staff to Mullah Omar, the head of the Taliban, so his signature carried great authority. (He is currently their minister of foreign affairs.)

Funding was the first problem. To maintain my impartiality, I needed funding from a third party not connected to either the Taliban or the Northern Alliance. Foundations had given up on Afghanistan. An officer from the Soros Foundation told me that if the Afghans really wanted peace, they could work it out on their own. This revealed his cynicism as well as his lack of appreciation for what a mediator does. In the end, I got money from friends who continue to think I may do good.

This was to be another low-budget operation. I flew out of New York on Halloween night, 1997, for seven months in Afghanistan. The first stop was Pakistan, a stepping stone to Afghanistan, and the base for United Nations and NGO operations in Afghanistan.

In Islamabad, the first thing I did was to buy a copy of the Koran and a small book called *Ninety-Nine Names of Allah*. I had entered the realm of Islam, and it was important to reconnect with the culture. In law school I took a course in Islamic law, but that was years ago. According to tradition, the Koran was revealed to the prophet Muhammad by the Archangel Gabriel during the Prophet's meditations in a mountain cave. Islamic law is rooted in the Koran and branches out in the sayings and acts of Muhammad, and then to authoritative rulings of Islamic jurists.

Fundamentalism has given Islam a bad name, especially regarding militancy and woman's rights, and it is the dominant force in the Taliban movement. But fundamentalism is a very small part of Islam. Muhammad was a reformer, who gave rights to women and orphans who had never enjoyed rights before, who preached compassion in the form of charity and forgiveness, and who taught tolerance in the form of religious freedom. It was this spirit of reform and human rights in the Islamic culture that I wanted to review.

Some Islamic scholars say there are three thousand names of Allah. One thousand are known by angels; one thousand are known by the prophets; nine hundred are in the Bible; ninety-nine in the Koran; and one is a secret name, the "greatest name of Allah." The ninety-nine names of Allah are used for worship. The idea is that each name represents a certain quality of God. If one repeats a certain name, then it invokes that quality and infuses it into the soul. Thus if one repeats Ya-Rahim (The Merciful), one becomes a friend of all. This same practice is found in Hinduism, with its thousand names of Mother Divine and countless other mantras. The practice is based on the universal belief that the soul has its roots in one source of life (God), from which it draws its energy and wisdom. The ninety-nine names plug you into the source. The Koran and the *Ninety-Nine Names of Allah* gave me the spiritual focus to relate to the Afghan culture.

From Islamabad, I took a bus to the city of Peshawar on the Afghan border. Nearing Peshawar, we passed through a small town that had a whole block of stores selling AK-47 assault rifles. This was my first sign of Afghanistan. An older gentleman sitting next to me kept speaking in a language I could not place. He showed me his card that read "Former Member of the Parliament of Afghanistan." I showed him my invitation letters. He invited me to his home, where his wife fed me and gave me traditional Afghan clothing to wear (baggy pants secured by a draw string and a loose-fitting shirt that flows down past the knees). "The Taliban do not like jeans," she told me with a giggle. The AK-47s and the hospitality are two aspects of Afghanistan that I would see everywhere in Afghanistan: the dichotomy of war and profound friendliness.

The next morning found me at the International Red Cross headquarters in Peshawar to catch a flight to Kabul. The Red Cross has its largest operation in Afghanistan and keeps a few planes for operational support. They provide free flights for journalists and anyone involved in NGO work. Without the Red Cross it would have been impossible for me to travel in Afghanistan.

KABUL WAS IN rubble. Years of civil war had devastated the city. But when I arrived the situation was calm. The Taliban had taken Kabul a year earlier, and the Northern Alliance had a policy of not shelling the place. The first thing a Westerner notices in Kabul are the *chaderis* (or *burkas*) all the women wear by order of the Taliban. Chaderis are loose-fitting garments that cover a woman from head to toe, with a small fishnet opening for them to see out of. No telling who is underneath. It could be a defiant young woman with blue hair, wearing lipstick and a tight miniskirt. It could even be a man. I heard a story of a man arrested for "impersonating" a woman by wearing a chaderi. In Taliban territory, all men are mandated to wear beards and traditional clothing.

The purpose of the chaderi is to protect woman from lust. But the psychological effect is more complex. Woman find ways of making the chaderi sexy, such as making it silklike to conform to the contours of the body when the wind blows. And men, accustomed to the chaderi, are easily influenced by simple innuendoes in body language. After months of seeing nothing but chaderis, the sight of a young woman on the street with a bare face knocked me over.

In conversation one day, the deputy of protocol asked me what I thought of their weather. His accent (and perhaps my frame of mind) made "weather" sound like "woman." I said, "Your women? Sure I like them just fine." "No! no!" he said. "Weather! Weather! Not woman." It was a delicate issue for them, but we couldn't help but laugh.

A Westerner is also struck by the manner of greeting. Afghans greet by placing the right hand over the heart and saying "*ah salam ali koom*," a universal Muslim greeting meaning "peace (salam) be with you." That is sometimes followed by questions about your health and family and a brisk handshake. Almost as common is the saying "*inshallah*," meaning "God willing." Whenever there is an agreement, for example to meet the next morning, or any opinion regarding the future, it will be followed by "inshallah." Westerners tend to consider this as a indication of noncommitment and are sometimes irritated. But this is not the case. It is the Afghan's deeply rooted belief that much of life is outside of human will, that God's will permeates all. In earlier centuries, "God-willing" was a common saying in the West, but it has lost its usage.

The final most evident thing is the presence of the UN and NGOs, made visible by their vehicles—often Toyota Land Cruisers—with painted insignias and flying flags. Most NGOs are highly effective organizations, with motivated personnel working for modest salaries. The most impressive of these is the Red Cross and Doctors Without Borders, who, at great risk, provide a healing hand to victims of war and natural disaster. The UN is much more of a mixed bag. It does do good things. On the other hand, the UN tends to attract people motivated by getting large salaries and pensions, resulting in a sluggish, ineffective, and sometimes corrupt bureaucracy.

A U.S. businessman visiting Kabul told me that when he was in Somalia, a high UN official offered him a sum of money to help him get a fortune out of the country he had stolen from the UN. The offer was rejected, but the money got out and the official is still working for the UN.

ONE NIGHT I stayed up late chatting with a couple of guys. One was a Somali doctor working for the UN; the other was a retired Scottish soldier working with the UN to rid the Afghan landscape of mines and unexploded bombs. The Taliban prohibit alcohol but give some leeway to Westerners. So these two were drinking up a storm. Because I was a single American not associated with any organization, and yet meeting with Afghan officials, they were convinced I was with the CIA. When I told them that I didn't drink, the Scot asked me whether it was because I did not want to get drunk, relax my defenses, and reveal my "mission." He repeated it a couple of times before I realized he was serious.

Among the many subjects discussed was the nature of the soul. I said the soul was immortal and passed through myriad lifetimes until it perfected itself and became like a column in the mansion of God. The Somali said that the soul stayed in a type of limbo after death until Judgment Day, when God separated the good from the bad. The Scot wondered if we actually believed these things; then he promoted his theory that we are dust but achieve immortality by passing our genetic material to our progeny. The Somali did not understand him. I told the Somali that it was some form of ancestor worship, which he understood (being from Africa), but which irritated the Scot.

As the night burned, words became more slurred and

thinking more foggy. The Scot, getting on in years, decided to show that he still had great strength. He took his shirt off to display his barrel chest and challenged the Somali doctor to a friendly wrestling match. The Somali reluctantly accepted, and I watched in amusement as they thrashed about. The Somali put the Scot in a headlock, and the Scot went completely nuts, throwing the Somali around and turning the match into a serious life-and-death struggle.

The Scot, after calming down a bit, explained that he thought he had been in a "death" hold where his neck could have been broken. The Somali felt insulted by being thrown around and being misjudged as actually trying to kill the Scot. He told me later that he would like to put the Scot in a large fire and "poke him around." Their relationship never fully recovered. Alcohol has been by far the most destructive of "recreational" drugs, and I could understand the Taliban's objection to it, though not their methods of policing it.

I spent one day walking around Kabul with a British doctor who was doing consulting work for the UN. He was upset about the Taliban policy of keeping the faces of women shrouded while being treated by male doctors. The eyes, he told me, are essential to look at for diagnosing an illness. During our walk, we found ourselves on a remote dirt road, where for about four city blocks, there was nothing but firewood for sale. A group of about seven rugged-looking men stood together, staring at us with furrowed brows. The doctor approached them with an open hand and a big smile, turning them into smiling children. We talked a bit in different languages and went on our way.

The doctor explained to me that in his many travels around the world, whenever he comes across such a group of men, he always goes up to the toughest, meanest looking guy and befriends him. He has been traveling all his life and he was well into his seventies, so it seems to have worked well for him.

The episode with the Scot and Somali was a miniature of most human conflicts: illusion, leading to fear and violence. The episode with the British doctor was a miniature of most reconciliations: trust and an open hand.

The British doctor once asked me if I was married. I told him I was married once at the age of 24 but divorced two years later. The marriage resulted in two children, Leila and Gabriel. I have another daughter, Azure, from a high school sweetheart. That relationship also did not work out. But I have three beautiful children. The doctor thought it humorous that a mediator was divorced. It is something like a car mechanic with a car that never works.

I explained that mediation does not attempt simply to bring people together. More precisely, a mediator attempts to define the best form of relationship, which may be separation. The real focus is peace and harmony, not forced union. Afghanistan should develop some system that gives breathing room to the various ethnic and religious groups. The Taliban were attempting to force all the people in Afghanistan under one ideology, smothering out cultural differences. That will never work.

THE FIRST NIGHT I was in Kabul I had a nightmare of being in a earthquake with the building collapsing on me. I jumped out of bed and ran to the window, throwing my hands up to feel for an opening before I realized it was just a dream. A few days later I had a nightmare of soldiers breaking into my room. Because my dreams sometimes come true, I was a little concerned. But it is the calm waking mind that always has the final say for me. Dreams are symbolic and are often simply a release of emotional tension.

As it turned out, during my stay in Afghanistan, there was a massive earthquake that killed about five thousand people. But I was not in it. Another earthquake of the same size occurred just after I left. And a guest house I was staying at in the north changed hands during fighting between two factions. But I was away at the time, and a servant was able to sneak my luggage away to his house for safekeeping.

Afghanistan was plagued by earthquakes, fighting, famine, flooding, bandits, and the severe pangs of poverty. But I saw little of this directly. Even the poverty was often hidden behind the thick mud walls of the homes. Mostly it was the beauty of Afghanistan that I saw: friendly people and lovely countryside.

Taliban on a Tiger

TALIBAN IS THE plural form of the word *talib*, meaning student, more specifically, religious student. There is a saying that if you want to start a revolution, go to the universities because students are energetic, idealistic, and often gullible. This is what the Taliban did. Many of the Taliban come from *madrasas* (Islamic schools) in Pakistan, where they were educated in fundamentalism and militancy. The Taliban arose in South Afghanistan as a movement to restore order in a countryside ruled by warlords and roaming bands of soldiers. They proved very successful, and the government in Kabul welcomed them until they began shelling Kabul and demanding the removal of the government.

The Taliban are primarily ethnic Pashtoons, making up 40 to 45 percent of the population. Other major groups in Afghanistan are the Tajiks, Uzbeks, and Hazara (a Shia Muslim minority), making up much of the Northern Alliance. For two hundred and fifty years before the communist coup in 1978, the Afghan government was ruled by Pashtoons, with the Tajiks making up most of the bureaucracy and the Hazara on the bottom of the social ladder, invariably oppressed. The Taliban want to restore the dominance of the Pashtoon, and the other ethnic groups have rejected this, seeking a more democratic process.

The political and military factions therefore follow ethnic lines. But there is a lot of spillover with Pashtoons in the Northern Alliance and with other ethnic groups under the Taliban. The conflict has little to do with ethnic hatreds. It has more to do with power relations and fundamentalist ideology. Outside of politics, ethnic groups mix together very well.

My first meeting in Kabul with a Taliban official was with Deputy Minister Stanakzai. He had a sparse beard that was not up to the expectations of the Taliban code for a full beard. But he spoke excellent English and was an equally excellent spokesperson for the Taliban. He gave a long presentation, which I reduced in my mind to three points: the Northern Alliance had their chance to bring peace to Afghanistan, but failed; a coalition government between the Taliban and the Northern Alliance is not possible; and the only path to peace is the defeat of the

Northern Alliance through war. As a mediator, this left me little to work with.

When the mujahadeen took power in 1992, they formed a government with the hopes of restoring peace. But civil war engulfed them. This was partly because of jealous rivalries among the mujahadeen, but the primary reason was Pakistan. Pakistan has a large population of Pashtoons and a long-standing policy of supporting a Pashtoon-dominated government in Afghanistan. They believe (wrongly, I think) that a Pashtoon-dominated government could give them more influence in Afghan affairs regarding Central Asia and especially Kashmir. Pakistan originally put their support behind a Pashtoon group led by an ambitious leader by the name of Hekmyatar. It was Hekmyatar who shelled Kabul for years, reducing it to the rubble I found when I arrived. Pakistan eventually withdrew their support from Hekmyatar and put it behind the Taliban.

I did not raise these points. As a mediator, my first priority is to listen and try to understand. My second priority is to make suggestions that may take root and sprout into policy. An academic would have engaged Stanakzai in a heated discourse. I looked for a point to agree on: "I agree. A coalition government would not work. It would only be an invitation for a continued civil war," I said. His jaw dropped. He was astonished that I agreed with him, because Western policy endorsed a coalition government. "There is too much jealousy and animosity between the leaders," I added.

I suggested a federal system, where each side would continue to govern their own territory but elect a government with powers limited to foreign affairs. As they grew in confidence in the government, they could delegate more powers to it. Because the Taliban had few foreign affairs links (only Pakistan, Saudi Arabia, and the United Arab Emirates recognized them), they would lose little. Stanakzai listened but did not comment. This is to be expected. It would be dangerous for him express a personal opinion on policy.

My next meeting was with Mullah Mutaqi, a minister in the ruling council, a type of cabinet of Mullah Omar, head of the Taliban. All Taliban leaders are called *mullah*, meaning religious teacher, though their training is often very limited. Religion, as mentioned, is a source of authority for the Taliban. Mutaqi was in his late twenties. He was friendly and exercised considerable power in the Taliban movement.

I presented a peace plan that allowed the Taliban to represent Afghanistan at the UN but called for a constitutional convention to form a new government. I knew the Northern Alliance would not accept the Taliban representing Afghanistan at the UN (they currently represent Afghanistan), but I thought they might be willing to share the responsibility as a stepping-stone to reconciliation. My purpose was to see if there were any conditions in which the Taliban might relinquish power to a new government. So I presented the most favorable plan. To my surprise, Mutaqi accepted all the points. The interpreter, who worked for him was really excited, saying to me with glee, "He agrees! He agrees!" as we were walking from the meeting.

Most impressive were the Taliban civil servants in Kabul. These people are a mix of ethnic groups that had served under a number of governments. They tolerated the Taliban policies, quietly complained about the poverty, sometimes joking about the beards and other religious laws, and supported any and every peace process. They represented the average Afghan who, very tired of twenty years of war, wanted peace and reconciliation.

AFTER A ONE-WEEK trip to the North where I met with the leaders of the Northern Alliance, I returned to the South, this time to Kandahar, the power center of the Taliban and of their leader, Mullah Omar. The Northern Alliance gave a tentative green light on a proposed plan I drafted where foreign affairs would be shared and a constitutional assembly formed. Because Mullah Omar never met with westerners, I met with Wakhil Ahmad, Mullah Omar's spokesman, who tore the plan to pieces. He considered the Northern Alliance to be a minority opposition party, claiming they held only 15 percent of the territory. Actually, it was closer to one-third, but territory itself is not an accurate way to measure the significance of a political or military force. Wakhil Ahmad seemed willing to accept the Northern Alliance as a small minority opposition party *within* the Taliban but not as an equal partner.

The next meeting was with the governor of Kandahar. The first thing I noticed about the governor was his missing leg. He was injured fighting the Soviets, resulting in an on-the-spot amputation, followed by a two-day trip on a donkey to Pakistan for treatment. The governor is known for having a bad temper. During a meeting sometime after I left, he got so angry with a UN official that he slapped him and followed this up by throwing a chair and teapot at him. I cannot imagine what the UN official said to provoke such a response, nor how the governor managed to balance himself on one leg to do this. In my experience it is attitude, that is, how you say something that matters most. A condescending, paternalistic, self-righteous, or haughty air will get anyone angry, whether they show it or not. Most anything can be discussed if approached in a respectful manner.

I got along well with the governor. I began by bringing up some basic points in Islam regarding political philosophy. One is that Islam endorses leaders who do not lust or aspire for power. The governor looked at me and said, "Yes, true, I didn't want this job. It was pushed on me." I believed him. There is little money involved. He's so poor that he wears the same thing every day, washing it at night for the next morning.

There is also little government money or political will to implement policy. When I was there he was trying to bring women back into the workplace because of the severe poverty in Kandahar. But he was unable to do so because of the opposition of the religious police, who think that women should not go to school or work. The governor spoke to me in deep, heartfelt tones about the poverty and sorrow the war has caused. The guy was genuine.

I pointed out that Islam endorses the use of assemblies to resolve disputes and that leaders must be loved by the people. These two points support a democratic process for reconciliation. The governor agreed. He told me that the Taliban would accept my proposals or other variations of an assembly if the Ulema (council of Islamic scholars) recommended it.

The Taliban were pushing the use of the Ulema to resolve the conflict. The idea was that a council of Islamic scholars from both sides would get together and decide on a path for peace. Whatever the decision, the parties would have to abide by it. This was a sound process. The problem was that the Taliban were interested in the

Ulema answering only one question: Who was more Islamic, the Taliban or the Northern Alliance? They were hoping that the answer would go in their favor, giving them legitimacy. They were not using the council as a process of reconciliation but as an aid to gain control of Afghanistan. The Ulema process finally collapsed.

I WAS CONVINCED that the Taliban were divided into two camps. One camp wanted reconciliation, but this was mainly comprised of mid-level civil servants. The stronger camp, led by Mullah Omar, wanted to continue the war until they had control over Afghanistan. The challenge was to strengthen the moderate elements in the Taliban that wanted reconciliation in order to create a change of policy. This would not be easy.

The Taliban movement is fueled by fundamentalist zealots, who demand the enforcement of fundamentalist codes. This includes amputations of hands for petty theft, flogging women for adultery, prohibiting women from education and the workplace, prohibiting male doctors from touching the skin of women or looking into their eyes, prohibiting photographs of people, prohibiting video and music tapes, and forcing people to mosques for prayer. Mullah Omar once declared that President Clinton should be stoned to death for his adulterous relationship with Monica Lewinsky. If he was not serious, it would be funny.

Without the fundamentalists, the Taliban have no power. Thus when the governor wanted to bring women back into the workplace, he was stopped by the very people who keep him in power. And when Mullah Omar, the Taliban leader, approved a plan for establishing schools for girls, it was later withdrawn by him after the same resistance emerged. The Taliban are riding on the back of a tiger and cannot get off for fear of being eaten. They cannot end the war, because the fundamentalist element demands that it continue.

Religious fundamentalism, whether Islamic, Christian, or Hindu, is characterized by rigidity of thinking and intolerance of other beliefs. In this respect, it is the very opposite of spiritual development. The flowering of the soul is a process of constant renewal of thought; and the mind, tempered by an awakening compassion, tends to be tolerant and appreciative of other belief systems.

Traditionally, the Afghan culture was very tolerant of other religious traditions. This included not only other Muslim sects, but also Hindus, Sikhs, and Jews. As in Kashmir, one reason for this was the popularity of the undogmatic mysticism of Sufism. The rise of fundamentalism, specifically the Taliban, has reversed this trend of tolerance.

Fundamentalism, only as a system of belief, is rather harmless. However, when it turns down the road of fear and prejudice, it begins to be spiritually destructive. When it turns down the road of militancy, it reaches its nadir, falling into a whirlpool of coarse passions, far removed from the high ideals of religion.

The Taliban had become completely overshadowed by a passion of self-righteousness and conquest. The irony is that the source of the passion was religious. But the effect of the passion was that it overshadowed the rational mind and thus separated the Taliban from their own source of wisdom and from their connection to God.

Humans are creatures of habit; they tend to maintain the status quo. This conflicts with the underlying principle in life of evolution and change. So humans tend to be in constant struggle with nature as the undercurrents of life push, pull, squeeze, and beat humans into moving forward. Humans are always resentful about this, rarely realizing this is for their own benefit. This applies to both the individual and the society. We are born with well-defined characters that translate into habits, and we spend a lifetime trying to break them to evolve a more refined character with better habits. I spent lifetimes, I think, as a monk, and still do not fully feel at home in the world of action.

The Taliban, as a culture, are doing their best to hold on to their old cultural habits, including the violent imposition of their beliefs on others. But they are up against the wall. The larger world and the spiritual forces within their own souls no longer accept this mentality, pushing them to their own destruction.

ONE OF THE most basic lessons of the human race is to develop the rational mind. By rational I do not mean intellectual. I mean a mind where all the faculties—ego, intellect, emotions, and senses—are harmonized and balanced by the silent voice rooted in the ground of our being. In the West, the icon of the rational mind has often been Socrates, who could drink the poisonous hemlock during his execution while calmly discussing the immortality of the soul with his disciples.

There are days in the lives of all of us when no matter what obstacles face us, we seem to maintain an inner calm and make the wise decision, sailing through the storm with skill and ease. Few have this experience all the time. I do not think I have met anyone who has truly mastered this wisdom. For most of humanity, the voice of wisdom flickers faintly, often smothered by storms of emotions or by strong mental habits that drown out the subtle impulses of the mind. Conflicts, both inside a person and between people and nations, are mostly the result of the rule of emotions that enslave minds not yet refined or tamed by wisdom.

The struggle with the rational mind is also common among spiritual aspirants. Those with deep spiritual experiences often become so identified with the experience that they are fooled into thinking that all of their thoughts are somehow right and pure. They fail to see that their desires must still be tempered with reason and common sense. They forget that they are struggling like the rest us in developing the rational mind.

Enlightenment is the union of the soul with God. It is a long process in which the soul is purified, refined, and prepared to house a higher spiritual energy. It is the grand quest, and the development of the rational mind is one of the basic lessons on the way. Enlightenment is born within the corridors of ignorance. Spiritual experiences are moments when the soul is infused with a higher energy that shakes it up and pushes it forward. The object is not the experience, but the attainment. That is, it is what is incorporated in us as part of our nature. No matter how enlightened we think we may be, there is always the possibility of making the wrong decisions. We always have to be alert and on our toes.

I think the human mind is at an infant level of development, sprouting its first leaves. If we imagine a universe populated by intelligent life, where the most advanced life is at a doctorate level of life's schooling, I would guess that we are still in grade school or perhaps preschool.

However, a rational mind is a balanced mind, not necessarily a fully developed mind. We may have very small minds, but we are awake enough to attempt to balance them with wisdom.

There have been moments during meditation when vistas open up and I see vast spaces, mountains, forests, or the spinning earth. These are only brief moments. But it gives me a hint of what a more evolved mind may be like.

When I think of China, Tibet, Kashmir, or Afghanistan, I remember the people I talked with, places I saw, and articles I have read. But my conception is so vague and limited in scope. Imagine a higher mind, such as an angel, focusing its attention on one of these countries. It would directly perceive the whole country, penetrating into the thoughts of its countless people. This higher perception would not be vague memories of a few experiences, but a direct perception, perhaps reaching far back into history and forward into a projected future. It would be as if the higher mind had eyes and ears everywhere throughout the country. Its very being would stretch out through the land. Now, that is a mind. In contrast, ours is so very small and dim.

Human clairvoyance represents the first sproutings of such a higher mind. Clairvoyance is essentially a refinement of the senses. It is a faculty of perception whereby a person can sense the thoughts and feelings of others, can sense what is happening at far distances, can sense what has happened in the past and what may come to pass. But human clairvoyance is only a faculty. It is perception that must be filtered through an infant human mind.

Clairvoyant perceptions, vague in their infancy, are further modified by a mind often full of prejudice, fears, and anxieties. This is why I always tell people not to take clairvoyants too seriously. Clairvoyance, even when it is pure, is only a source of information, not a source of wisdom. What is important is not good perception, but good judgment. That is why the wise man is sometimes portrayed as blind. He is completely focused on the inner source of wisdom. The source of wisdom is not the clairvoyance, but the still inner voice that harmonizes and guides: the voice of wisdom rooted deep in our being.

The Taliban represent the most extreme human case of an overshadowed rational mind. They are so overwhelmed by passion and so focused on narrow interpretations of Islam that they have drowned out the one true guide to God that lies within them.

ISLAM ALLOWS TWO justifications for the use of force. The first is self-defense against an aggressor. The second is self-defense against religious oppression. This places Islam in accord with international law, which recognizes only self-defense, including collective self-defense and humanitarian intervention, as legitimate justifications for the use of force. The Universal Islamic Declaration of Human Rights was announced in 1981. Drafted by eminent Muslim scholars, it is also in accord with international standards, including women's rights. Islam, interpreted by rational minds, can become a strong spiritual pillar in the international community. But like Christianity, Hinduism, and Buddhism, when interpreted through violent passions, Islam becomes a pretext for hatred and violence.

The wise can extract from their own experiences the eternal truths of religion. But no amount of scripture can instantly instill wisdom in the unwise. It takes a long time. Scripture is meant to represent a record of communion between God and humans. Even if we accept it as such, scripture has its limitations.

One is that it is a communication to a particular people at a particular time. So even though there may be "universal" truths conveyed, much of the scripture may only apply to the special needs of the people of that time (not to all people at all times). However, the most fundamental limitation is that scripture is confined to a set of propositions—to the written word. The simple statement "God exists," may be understood by a small child, but it does not convey the experience of the vast beauty of God.

The wisdom of God is lost in print. This is because the wisdom resides in the direct experience of the vastness of the being of God. This vastness is lost when squeezed down to words, sentences, and books. These represent only old rickety signposts, pointing to a place where each of us will eventually bask in the warmth of that wisdom through direct spiritual communion. The highest form of communication with God is the direct *experience* of God. The soul merging with pure Spirit is the only way for the soul to fully appreciate the nature of God.

Communication with God may also come in visions through a type of thought transference far beyond the limitations of words. For a moment, you are lifted to a higher place, brilliant and full of joy, where your mind is a little closer to the divine mind and able to get a more accurate experience of this higher wisdom. When this happens, a person may struggle a lifetime to encapsulate the experience with human words, always falling short. I think God communicates to us in innumerable ways. But most fundamentally, I think this communication comes through our own awakening mind. This may be as deep and profound as our capacity allows.

There is a line in the Bhagavad-Gita saying that for an enlightened person, the Vedas (scripture) are of no more use than a well surrounded by water on all sides.

The Lion of Five Lions

THE NORTHERN ALLIANCE was composed of about five to seven factions, depending on how you count them. Each faction was headed by a strong leader, most of whom have fought each other at some time. The alliance was therefore fragile. But the factions of the alliance were distinguishable from the Taliban in that they all had a genuine desire for national reconciliation. They understood that no one group could dominate Afghanistan. This provided a small window of opportunity for a mediator. I decided to mediate a common policy for national reconciliation among the factions of the North.

A common policy would clarify their position to the Afghan people and to the world. It would also act as a rallying point to support a peace process. If enough support for a peace plan was obtained from the Afghan people and the international community, this could force a shift in Taliban policy from conquest and oppression to national reconciliation. This was the plan.

In practical terms, this meant a written agreement signed by all the members of the alliance. This would not be easy. I would have to draft an agreement, present it to the members, and edit it to fit the wishes of everyone. This would be difficult enough with only two parties involved. In the end, the agreement had nine signatures and took three months from conception to completion.

I began the work in Mazar-i-Sharif, the main city in the North. Mazar was divided among the various factions, each controlling a part of the city, so there was always tension. Guns were everywhere. Main intersections had small groups of soldiers sitting at tables with machine guns, watching the cars go by. The streets were full of young men walking around with AK-47s casually slung over their shoulders like college kids with backpacks.

The rocket-propelled grenades (RPGs) were another common sight. The RPG was a small aerodynamic explosive about the size of a man's foot with a two-foot-long shaft extended behind it. To fire it, the shaft was placed inside a bazooka-looking gun. Soldiers would carry extra RPGs on their backs like archers carrying arrows.

Soldiers rarely wore uniforms. Mostly it was traditional clothing: colorful turbans and long quilt dresses with candy-cane colors of reds and greens. Or it was dark brown wool "pajamas" flowing to below their knees and a checkered black and white (or red and white) cloth wrapped around their heads. The soldiers were usually kids, often uneducated and always friendly, and I never felt any danger walking the streets.

Most of the leaders were to be found in or around Mazar. I began the process with President Rabbani. Rabbani was the symbol of unity for the alliance and spent much of his time coordinating the factions. He approved my proposal and was eager for me to obtain the signatures. As president, he would sign last to give the document legal effect.

There was usually a certain amount of formality in these meetings. Tea and snacks were always served and often a cameraman would video it to be played on Mazar TV that evening along with other events of the day. In my meetings with Minister of Home Mohaqaq, his guards would give crisp salutes as I walked in and out of the gates. They knew I was there to help bring peace, and this was the way they showed their respect. Mohaqaq had also fought the Soviets. Soviets sometimes put antipersonnel mines under prayer rugs at mosques, and Mohaqaq accidentally set one off while praying. Luckily, he had suffered only minor injuries, because the rug was so thick it absorbed much of the blast.

Mustafa Qasemi was the biggest supporter of my efforts in Mazar. He was the leader of a small but influential Hasara military and political group. He was young for a leader (around thirty) and was always happy and full of energy. He told me, "Military commanders come to me for hire and I tell them that I cannot pay them as much as the big leaders can. But they say, 'We don't mind. We like you because you're so funny.'" He was. He made a sharp contrast with the typical commander who wore a grim face and barked orders. He wore no uniform and held his troops together with the bonds of friendship and respect. It was Qasemi who convinced Mohaqaq and acting Prime Minister Javid to put the first signatures on the document. And it was Qasemi who, when I ran out of money after spending months in northern Afghanistan, sent his assistant to give me five U.S. one-hundred-dollar bills.

But the real key to a successful document was the backing of Ahmad Shah Masood. He was the minister of defense for the alliance, but preferred the more simple title of "commander" Masood. He held the front line at Kabul against the Taliban and was the center of the alliance. Masood was a great hero in the Afghan fight against the Soviets. He would draw Soviet troops up the Panshir Valley and then counterattack and destroy them. He did this again and again and became an instrumental force in defeating them.

For this and because the Afghan war was instrumental to the fall of the Soviet Union, the *Wall Street Journal* once called Masood "The Afghan who won the Cold War." But for the Afghans, Masood became known as the "Lion of Panshir." Panshir means five lions, so it translates as the lion of five lions. There is an old Afghan saying that anyone who wants to conquer Afghanistan should beware, because under every rock of every mountain lies a sleeping lion. When Masood was fighting the Soviets, they said, "And the lion is Ahmad Shah Masood."

MASOOD'S OFFICE AND home were in Panshir Valley, hundreds of miles from Mazar. Masood arranged for me to fly from Mazar to Panshir in one of his helicopters. It was an old Soviet military transport helicopter, modified with red Afghan carpets on the floor and red-cushioned arm chairs. Flying over the Hindu Kush Mountains in winter provided a show of vast carpets of snow sparkling in the sun. Occasional valleys were still green, with herds of goats moving about like little toys on the hillsides. Some of these valleys are so remote that villages there may exist for hundreds of years without interference from the changing world outside.

On arrival, I was taken on a long drive through the valley to one of Masood's guest houses. Panshir Valley was spotted with villages of well-dressed and friendly people, living in cottages with gardens, as goats roamed the hillsides. The facial characteristics and hairstyle of the men reminded me of ancient Greeks and Romans. I later learned that Alexander the Great had marched up this valley, leaving behind many of his men who had suffered from snow blindness. The merging of cultures over two thousand years ago could still be felt. The valley was idyllic, with a crystal-clear stream running down the middle and lofty mountains on each side. Along the river every fifty yards or so were wrecked Soviet tanks and armored vehicles, like museum pieces reminding everyone of the ten years of war against the Soviets.

Because it was winter and there was no electricity in the valley other than that provided by personal generators, the rooms of the guest house I was taken to were heated by wood stoves. These filled the room with the scent and sounds of burning wood. After a "special" meal and the customary green tea and much chatting, I began to fall asleep in my chair. At about ten o'clock, I heard the faint announcement: "Now entering is Ahmad Shah Masood." No one was expecting him until the next day. As I rose, he walked in with the presence of a king, smiling graciously. He was a master of stealth and had a reputation of surprising people. Like Qasemi, Masood was not the typical military figure. He wore immaculate traditional civilian clothes, spoke politely, and laughed a great deal.

We talked until midnight. He had a clear vision for the future of Afghanistan, which consisted of a unified country under a democratic regime. He had talked to the Taliban leader Mullah Omar a few times over satellite telephone. Mullah Omar told him that the Afghan people were too ignorant for democracy and needed to be governed by someone like himself. Just months earlier, the Taliban had taken considerable amounts of territory and

Masood was the only obstacle to their victory. Mullah Omar offered him a sweet deal. Masood called his council together for a discussion. In council he placed his round wool hat on the table and, pointing to it, declared, "As long as I have this much territory I will fight." The Taliban were pushed back soon afterwards.

AFTER MY MEETING with Masood, I went to Jabulsaraj, a town just outside of Panshir Valley, for meetings with Masood's advisers. Jabulsaraj is a collection of villages. It is laced with crystal-clear streams branching off into smaller steams two feet wide that flow through the villages to provide homes with water and to moisten their many small gardens. Aside from Masood's advisers, I also spoke with shopkeepers, farmers, and soldiers during my many long walks in the villages and countryside.

I spent my time going back and forth between Jabulsaraj and Panshir. I was the only Westerner in the area except for Andreas, a Red Cross fellow based in Panshir. He would drive through sometimes and leave me a copy of the *Economist*. So everyone wanted my ear to express their hopes and gripes with the West. Everyone considered the United States to be the backer of Pakistan, which backed the Taliban. It was hard for me to convince them otherwise. Fortunately, they did not blame me and, oddly, still held a love for America. The villagers would express their deep appreciation for what I was doing. They would encourage me, advise me, and constantly thank me. It was this connection with the people of Afghanistan that maintained my desire to follow through and do something of value.

Winter meant snow, and snow meant snow fights. Villagers in this area were masters in the use of the ancient sling used by David against Goliath. They would put a snowball in the sling, do a long swing or two, and release it. If this is done right, the sling will make a loud pop like a whip and the snowball will create a whizzing sound as it flies through the air at great speed. I spent hours watching these snow fights and once got hit in the shoulder. Even though I wore a heavy wool coat, it really stung, and the soldiers rocked with laughter. A solid hit by one of those snowballs in the head could put a man out cold. During the war with the Soviets, Afghan soldiers used the slings to throw grenades, usually down from a mountain. Now they were for play and the occasional use of the shepherd to guide his flock.

One day I saw a game of Afghan polo, called *buskashi*, played on the wide banks of the Panshir River. Essentially, this was a game of horseman fighting over a dead goat to see who can get it to one side of the field and back to the center. The horseman with the goat would carry it with one hand, using the other to maneuver his horse away from competing horseman trying to take it away from him. The champion was awarded prizes.

I was standing on the outskirts of the field, watching. Occasionally, horsemen would charge through the crowd, taking the game elsewhere for the moment, then rush back in. It was my first experience of being charged by a horseman. People around me would dart away, leaving me alone. I was afraid that if I tried to get out of the way, I might end up jumping in front of the horse. I just stood my ground, hoping the horse would not run me over. The power of this creature is immense. I now understand the terror foot soldiers felt when they faced a charging cavalry. Behind and above me on the hillside were children slinging snowballs. So I had to keep an eye out for horses in front of me and snowballs behind me.

A local newspaper published an article about me. It told of my trading candy for a sling and learning to use it. That made me famous. I gave lots of candy away until I began getting mobbed by hordes of children. Children played freely around the villages. They all knew me and would say "ah salam" to which I would often reply, "sad salam" (one hundred salams) or "lak salam" (one thousand salams) and they would giggle and run about. One day I heard children talking as they were walking behind me: "He's American," said one. "Yes," said another, "but he's Muslim." Meaning that, as American, I am suspect, but because I am a good person, I must be Muslim.

This area is famous for its bird hunting. Bird guns are a common sight, and people shoot birds in the middle of town. I'd be walking down the street and there would be a boom! Bird shot would patter around me. Even one of Masood's Taliban prisoners of war was once seen hunting birds, with the consent of the guards of course. I was often invited to hunt birds, but declined. A soldier once joked, "We Afghans do not mind shooting people, but he won't even shoot a bird!" I did shoot a can once. They were impressed because I shot standing without a brace and in a strong wind.

A BBC correspondent complained to me about all the guns in the area. He thought they were evidence of anarchy. I said, "Don't you know these are for bird hunting?" He was embarrassed by his lack of insight. Most of these guns were muzzle loaded and over one-hundred years old. Masood had taken them out of the king's storage and handed them out a few years ago. I tried to shoot one (a pistol), but it kept misfiring. This is why they are not used much any more except for bird hunting in Jabulsaraj and Panshir.

On clear days, Taliban planes would sometimes fly over and drop bombs. They flew too high to see, but the roar of the jet could be heard and then a distant boom. One day a few bombs landed in succession near me. Soldiers around me all jumped for cover, which led me to think the next would be on our heads. Instead, they hit a good hundred yards or more away and no one was hurt. There was also an occasional bullet that would fly over our heads with a whizzing sound, like a bumblebee going a few hundred miles an hour. The sound made me duck out of instinct, and the Afghans would tease me about it. On occasion, I would hear the low booms of large guns from the distant front. Once during a heavy offensive, the night sky lit up like lightning in distant clouds.

Months earlier, the Taliban had occupied Jabulsaraj. They had committed a lot of atrocities against the citizens in their attempts to force them to relocate. Some of the stories I heard are so gruesome I've never repeated them. The Taliban created so much animosity among the villagers that the Kabul front line is manned by volunteers from these and other villages in the area. A couple of months into my stay, some children took me to a clearing with bones. Pointing at the bones, they said, "Taliban." It was a warm spring day and the bones still had a moist life to them, giving off a slight odor. I had not known I was being taken there and was stunned by the sight. I paused for a moment and turned away in silent disgust. Fortunately, the real impact of the war never came too close to me. But there was always a distant reminder of the carnage.

When I viewed the poverty and the scars of war during my walks through the villages, there was always a silent follower. Ever present was my "pool of light," soothing me, bathing everything I saw with its brilliance. The contrast was stark: the deep serenity and beauty of the spiritual light and the mud streets full of people struggling to maintain a life, fearing the occasional bomb and the always-imminent invasion by the Taliban. The fear and pain of these people were real. But the spiritual light was also real. It was the white canvas that life is painted on; the eternal link with every soul's destiny and home. It gave me the inner calm needed to do the work I set out to do. No one wants a distraught mediator. If I am to talk about peace, I should at least have something of it in my soul.

I learned a lot about the culture and feelings of the Afghan people during these long walks through the villages. It was more a vacation than work: I enjoyed the beautiful mountains and streams, the friendly people, and the free time to reflect. As a child, I played a game of trying to look at things as if I was seeing them for the first time. For example, what if most of us had noses that stuck out three inches. What we now think of as an average nose would probably seem inadequate and ugly. Or what if, instead of twenty-four hour days, we had ten- or thirty-hour days? The idea was to challenge things that I took for granted and to look at the world with fresh eyes.

A big question for a mediator is why do people get along? Why is it that people can communicate? My answer is that we are rooted in a common spiritual source and thus share similar sensations, feelings, and thoughts. I came to Afghanistan as a stranger, but people could relate to me because I expressed the same thoughts and feelings that came from their hearts. With children, it is easy; a smile and a happy heart is enough. With adults, the feelings are more complex and the thought process more intricate. The important thing is the resonance. I resonated with something deep inside the Afghans: the desire for peace and harmony and an end to strife and injustice through a rational process. Whereas the first rule of war is deceit, the first rule of peace is honesty and an open heart that resonates.

The next question is why is there conflict? If we get along with each other because we have a common source, it follows that we do not get along because of the lack of a common source. Hate, anger, bigotry, suspicion, jealousy, greed, lust, and other variations of this theme are the big walls dividing us from this source. The development of love and sensitivity is the force to break through these walls. This is a matter of spiritual evolution, a long painful process of which we are all somehow part.

The walls dividing the Afghans were large and needed to be torn down. I thought an agreement among the factions interested in doing this would be a good start.

I SPENT TWO months going between Jabulsaraj and Panshir. When I left, the snow had melted and flowers were blooming everywhere. The reason I was there so long was that Masood wanted some changes in the document. It took about five meetings to get the document in order. In between meetings he was off dealing with the war and internal politics. But the end result was a refined document. Masood agreed with me on federalism but thought it should be decided by the constitutional assembly. The first order of things, he told me, was to establish a strong central government to prepare Afghanistan for democracy by collecting all the guns so that warlords would have no influence in elections. After that, a constitutional convention could be held.

My draft put emphasis on the constitutional assembly and the cooperative spirit between the central and local governments. The most important point was the willingness of the Northern Alliance to surrender power to persons who were not members of the alliance or of the Taliban, that is, "neutral" persons. With the "lion's" signature (three diagonal lines like lightning), the other signatures were guaranteed. I just had to go get them.

Before I left Panshir Valley, Masood invited me for breakfast at his home. In Afghanistan, meals are eaten on the floor, sitting on cushions around a cloth used like a table. The main dish was always *pilau*, a rice dish with beef. I had stopped eating beef as a teenager, but this was all I was served in Afghanistan. As a result, I gained a few pounds. The pilau was supplemented by small vegetable dishes and flat bread. People ate from the same dish with their hands, but I was always given my own plate with a spoon.

I had dinner with Masood once before, but this time was special. For one thing, it was breakfast, which meant no pilau. But more to the point, Masood wanted to share his political ideas with me. Masood spread the cloth out himself and served the food. It was a feast: marmalade, honey, carrot juice, orange juice, special teas, meats, eggs, various breads, fruits, and nuts. Spring air flowed into the room, and the morning sunlight splashed around the food. Peering out the window, I saw almond trees in full bloom and heard birds chirping. I told Masood that he had a beautiful garden. He told me that the Soviets had destroyed most of the trees. These had been planted after they left. When peace comes, there were other plans for electricity and reforestation of the mountainsides.

After the meal, Masood sat back and made a long presentation on his policy. I wrote it down in my notebook, occasionally asking him to clarify a point. The translator was former Vice President Mohtat, who held office under the last Soviet-supported regime. Masood was the key player in overthrowing that regime. So they were once enemies. But now Mohtat supported Masood, as many others do who had once fought against him.

Masood explained that the United States had initially supported the Taliban. He was not convinced that their policy had changed and wanted to emphasize the need for them to reconsider. He wanted to establish good relations with the United States and Pakistan and emphasized that he would rid Afghanistan of all terrorists and drug production.

Under the Taliban, Afghan drug production had become the largest in the world, and the international terrorist Osama bin Laden was under their care. "Bin Laden is a big problem," I pointed out. "He has the money to buy a nuclear bomb and float it up the Potomac River to Washington." Masood nodded in agreement.

Masood wanted to establish a regime where no one group would dominate others. It was a vision of democracy, human rights, and peace. I told him that the Taliban were bent on conquest and oppression, that the Northern Alliance was the single force for reconciliation, and that he was the person holding the alliance together. This made him the key to Afghan peace and reconciliation. "Tashakor" (thank you), he said. "Tashakor!" I replied.

Seeds of Peace

WITH DOCUMENT IN hand I returned to Mazar. While I was gone, there had been some fighting between the northern factions for control of Mazar, so I was put in a different guest house for safety. This guest house was the home of a wealthy merchant who did business with the faction leaders. In one transaction I watched, his servants unloaded large duffel bags full of Afghan currency in 10,000 Afghani notes (each worth about 60 cents); I calculated the total to be the equivalent of about 250,000 U.S. dollars. Late afternoons I spent playing badminton with the merchant's children and military guards in the rose garden. But my days were mostly spent getting the signatures on the document.

Around this time, Bill Richardson, the U.S. ambassador to the UN, was planning a trip to Afghanistan along with an entourage of American diplomats. The Americans were thinking of meeting a couple of Northern Alliance leaders separately. Acting Prime Minister Javid and Mustafa Qasemi complained to me that their political parties were being excluded. "We are part of the alliance and should be part of the talks," they told me. Promising them I would try to resolve this, I called the U.S. consul in Pakistan and discovered that the main consideration of the Americans was time. They had time for only a couple of meetings.

I set up a meeting with President Rabbani in Mazar to discuss the issue. When I arrived, the receptionist at the guard post left for a few moments and returned to say that the president was busy and I might have to wait quite a while. I knew he had not conveyed the message to the right people, and time was of the essence. So I just walked through the guard post. I was speaking harshly. The receptionist began yelling. Guns and people were stirring all around me. This got the attention of a senior presidential aid. I calmed everyone down, and explained myself again—that I had an important appointment. The aid conveyed my request and I was sitting with the president ten minutes later. A more skilled mediator would have been able to get through without the ruckus. But that was the best I could do at the time.

I recommended to the president that he request that the Americans have one meeting with representatives of all of the alliance members assembled together. This way, time would be saved, and no one would be excluded. Also the alliance would be seen as unified instead of factionalized. He agreed, and his secretary made the request. The Americans agreed, and the meeting was set at a place called Shebergan, located a couple hours drive west of Mazar, where General Dustom, the Uzbek leader, was based.

I also had to go there to get Dustom's signature. Dustom had a large palace in which I stayed for a few days. It had flower gardens and male peacocks that danced for their disinterested mates. A great number of people came through to visit Dustom. I met a boy of fourteen, who looked me up and down, asked about me, then shook my hand. He was quite confident and serious. It turns out that his father, a big commander, had been killed a year earlier in factional fighting.

Dustom, in respect to the boy's father, gave him his father's command of a few thousand soldiers. I watched the boy with interest during those days. He walked the palace grounds with authority. When he gave orders, they were immediately obeyed, and when he approached other commanders, they responded with respect. This little boy had command and authority, and he exercised it, without any adult adviser directing him.

I got Dustom's signature at midnight, the night before the Americans arrived. By ten o'clock the next morning, the streets of Shebergan were lined with soldiers and citizens to greet the Americans. These people stood out under a hot sun until about four o'clock, when the Americans finally showed up late. The Americans made quite a contrast from myself. They came in three planes— two for diplomats and staff and one for journalists. I was just a single person with my Afghan assistant, Philistine, so named because his grandfather came from Palestine.

Philistine was appointed to me by the Foreign Affairs Department of the Northern Alliance to guide, arrange meetings, translate, and generally keep me out of trouble. Without him, I would have been lost. Philistine was growing a full beard, because he had seen Mazar taken twice by the Taliban and wanted to be in good standing with them if they took Mazar again. He went everywhere with me, on long walks and hikes and to most of my meetings. He was something of a squire, attending my needs, defending my cause, and articulating my arguments.

Like many Moslems, Philistine was faithful in doing his five daily prayers. I often did my prayer/meditations in his company. He referred to my practice as a "free religion," because I could pray at any time, for any length, and in any manner I wanted. "I wish I had your religion," he said with a laugh.

WHEN THE SOVIETS left Afghanistan, Afghans expected the U.S. to help them, but the U.S. did not. In the eyes of most Afghans, America abandoned them after the

Afghans had helped America win the Cold War. Even so, Afghans remain forever hopeful that America will offer a helping hand. It was this hope in the eyes of the Afghans that I saw when the Americans came. Sadly, the American trip was little more than "photo-op diplomacy," as a former U.S. congressman later told me.

The Afghans expected a lot from the Americans, but got little. The UN already had a general agreement from the Taliban and Northern Alliance for talks. The United States came in to pressure them to set a date. Because the Taliban wanted U.S. support, they agreed to talks. The alliance, of course, also agreed. The problem was that there was no basis for talks. The Taliban was still resolved to take control of all of Afghanistan by force. Yes, they would talk, but they had no intention of pursuing reconciliation with the North. Forcing talks under these circumstances was foolish.

As I told a journalist, the old saying applies here: you can take a horse to water but you can't make him drink. The Americans had done no groundwork diplomacy to prepare the basis for talks. What was needed, as everyone knew, was a change of policy in the Taliban. Talks did occur in Pakistan between the Taliban and the Northern Alliance, but there was nothing to talk about, and as the war began to rage at new heights, the talks collapsed.

As the Americans flew from Sheldergan with their agreement and CNN coverage, I left for Mazar with Philistine by a rickety old taxi. It is a pleasant drive alongside fields of wild red poppies swaying in the breeze. Occasionally you would see children on the side of the road, filling in holes with whatever they could find. Travelers would throw money out of their windows as they sped by, as if offering a voluntary tax. I would let loose some bills and watch the air currents swish the money around as the children raced to catch it. In an earlier trip on this road, a soldier jumped out in front of the taxi and pointed his AK-47 directly at us in a threatening manner. It was not a good feeling. It turned out that he just wanted a ride. The taxi driver turned him down, and to my surprise, the soldier meekly consented.

In Mazar I obtained the final signature by President Rabbani, giving legal effect to a very different agreement than the one the Americans left with. It was an agreement only between the leaders of the northern factions, but it was genuine. All nine leaders who signed meant it. The title was fitting: "Framework for Peace for the People of Afghanistan." The document provided the framework, or seed form, for national reconciliation, and it was flexible enough for all Afghans. That is, all except for the funda-mentalist zealots inside the Taliban who rejected the underlying premise of reconciliation.

I had three documents with original signatures. One I left with President Rabbani. The second I took to the Taliban in Kabul and presented to Minister Mutaqi, who was very impressed by the fact that I was able to get all the signatures. "This must have been a very big job," he said. The third I gave to the UN Special Mission to Afghanistan at their office in Islamabad, Pakistan.

They had been watching my work. They agreed that the Taliban were committed to war and were frustrated in their own peace initiatives, which, with the help of the United States, fell flat.

Copies of the agreement were given to Western diplomats in Islamabad who, without embassies in Afghanistan, were in charge of the Afghan issue for their governments. I also gave copies of the "Framework" to journalists and other Afghan organizations based in Pakistan. I was spreading the "Framework" like Johnny Appleseed spreading apple seeds, but these were seeds of peace.

The acting British high commissioner (their term for ambassador) told me: "It's amazing that you have become an expert on Afghanistan in less than two years." I replied, "It's only because I spent time inside Afghanistan." Otherwise it is just armchair expertise. A mediator's expertise is mediation. Thrown into any conflict, a mediator can quickly uncover the forces at play without being an expert on the history or anthropology of the people involved.

The most basic forces preventing reconciliation were Pakistani military and logistical support for the Taliban and the militant fundamentalism that was the backbone of the Taliban movement. This support came mostly through Pakistan's Inter-Services Intelligence agency, which often acted independently from other parts of the Pakistan government. This support was complicated by thousands of Pakistani militants joining the ranks of the Taliban; and by funding from fundamentalists in Saudi Arabia to the Taliban and to Pakistani fundamentalist groups. Everyone knew this. The solution was strong pressure on Pakistan and the Taliban by the United States and other Western powers. But there was little political will for this.

At this time U.S. policy was still based on Cold War thinking in which Pakistan was a friend of the United States in its fight against an expansionist Soviet Union. The United States poured three billion dollars in arms for Afghans to fight the Soviets. Most of this money was channeled by Pakistan to fundamentalists. After the Cold

War, the United States maintained a policy of leniency toward Pakistani support of fundamentalist militants in Kashmir and Afghanistan, allowing for a monster to grow.

After I had returned to the United States, I got a letter from the State Department saying that they encouraged me to stay in contact with them so that I could share my ideas with them on where to go from here. I had sent them my analysis, but there was not much else I could offer. The international terrorist bin Laden has had a stronger impact in influencing policy.

Before I left for America in June 1998, bin Laden gave his now infamous news conference in Afghanistan in which he declared war on all Americans. This statement marked the pinnacle of militancy that has been flourishing in this area for so long. It revealed a deep spiritual sickness. In some way, it seemed as if he was raising his head to provoke a response and be killed. The U.S. policy of leniency came to haunt America with the bombings of the U.S. embassies in Africa not long after I left Afghanistan. The U.S. response of a cruise missile attack on the camps of bin Laden's network put a new element into the Afghan drama. Two of these camps were used for training Pakistanis for fighting in Kashmir.

This was a wakeup call for U.S. policymakers. Their old policy of looking the other way when Pakistan supports militant fundamentalism appeared to be over. But it took almost a year after the bin Laden affair before the State Department finally changed its policy and openly declared its opposition to Pakistan's support of the Taliban. This was a year during which many people, including myself, lobbied for such a change. Still, little has been done by the U.S. to curb the rise of militant fundamentalism in Afghanistan and Pakistan.

The seeds of war planted decades ago during the Afghan war with the Soviets are now bearing fruit. Afghanistan and Pakistan have become sanctuaries for fundamentalists promoting a global war, spreading across into China's Xinjiang province, Uzbekistan, Tajikistan, Kyrgyzstan, Chechnya, and other areas in the world. Out of the ashes of this war, the seeds of peace will eventually sprout. And the seeds of peace that I and others helped spread may find purpose.

After I returned to the United States, the Taliban swept through Dustom's area, where I am sure the boy commander put up a strong fight before being defeated. Mazar was taken and my Hazara friends fled. Thousands of ethnic Hazara were executed by the Taliban in Mazar, many in front of their families in a ritualistic slitting of throats. Jabulsaraj was taken by the Taliban, then retaken by Masood. Other areas were also taken by the Taliban, resulting in thousands of refugees fleeing in all directions. At this time (1999), Masood, in his stronghold in Panshir, again remains the last great obstacle to the Taliban. The Afghan drama, fueled by a bloodlust in the name of holiness, continues to play out.

BACK IN AMERICA, I went to my parents' home in Florida to rest. One day during meditation, as sometimes happens, I merged into a beautiful golden light. I was immersed in it as in a pool of water, with my head far below the surface. In fact, the light had the quality of liquid. It was golden liquid light, and my soul was saturated in it. Normally, I see the light shining from my spiritual sun, reminding me of my destiny as a human soul, but still feeling stained by my own inadequacies.

Now I was immersed in that light, and all sense of limitations vanished. There was only peace and bliss. As I came back to my normal state, I felt soothed and refreshed.

Spirituality is my first and central aspiration, and this experience made me reflect on the reasons I had engaged myself in such large human problems as Afghanistan, Tibet, Kashmir, and Burma. The original inspiration seemed faint and distant to me. As a boy, I spent some summer days at the beach fighting with the waves of the Atlantic Ocean. Occasionally a big wave would hit me and send me tumbling over an ocean floor of sand and rock. After a couple hours of fighting the waves, being burnt by the sun, and swallowing salt water, I was exhausted and had to retire. The waves, unaffected by my efforts, continued to roll in as they had for millions of years. Looking back on my peacemaking work made me feel just this way. What effect I have had on these issues, I do not know. But at least I jumped in and made an effort. And like the boy who returns to fight the waves the next day with refreshed energy, I may jump back into the fray again one day.

Such moments of reflection invoke the question of destiny. The concept of destiny is as old as the hills. So is the concept of free will. Destiny is linked to the idea of law. If the universe is governed by laws, then everything is determined by these laws, and life unfolds in a preordained fashion, like a movie on the big screen. Free will is tied to our subjective experience of being able to choose. If we all have free will, then human life unfolds in any direction in which our innumerable choices direct it. Thus a conflict arises: our deep notion of law implies destiny, but our equally deep sense of inner freedom implies free will.

The human mind, disliking conflicts, attempts to harmonize these two opposing concepts. Common experience suggests that life is a mixture of fate and free will. Some things in life seem set and inevitable: our birth, the character we are born with, and the circumstances into which we are born. These conditions set us in a general direction.

Alexander the Great was born the son of a king, was educated to be a soldier and a king, and had the character and passion to excel in this profession. When his father was murdered, he became king at the age of twenty and continued the conquests his father began. There was, we can imagine, no consideration in the young Alexander's mind as to whether or not to be king. It was a given and had all the characteristics of fate. His life was swept away by the forces of the times and by his own inner impulses. However, many of the decisions he made during his short reign involved considerable soul searching and choosing. Many biographies read this way, where either the circumstances of life or the character of the person weigh so heavily as to compel a certain result, a certain fate.

Following the theory that life is a mixture of free will and destiny, destiny deals with the larger things in life, while free will deals with the details. We may be "destined" to go to China or India to learn certain things, but we may "choose" to go in one year or another, to go by boat or plane, or to go alone or with someone else. The many decisions we make each day have an impact in the direction of our life, pushing it forward or backward, this way or that. But somehow, whichever way our free will takes us, we keep to the general plan and get the mission done. Ideally, of course, we want to live it as best as possible.

Theories of the doctrine of reincarnation and karma are often consistent with this experience of a mixture of fate and free will. When the soul is on the "other side" and about to enter a new life, it is infused with a higher wisdom and sees the "big picture," the grand design, as clearly as it is capable. It also sees its responsibilities for what it has put in motion in past lives as well as its need as a soul for further development. Within these set boundaries and tempered by a higher wisdom, the deep longing of the soul is let loose in choosing a life for itself.

The more evolved the soul is, the more freedom it has in choosing. The decision made is what we call "fate." We are like actors who become involved with the author in writing the script, then incarnate to play the role, forgetting we ever worked with the author. Thus, according to this theory, much of what we call fate is our own choosing, creating a marriage between fate and free will.

Our destiny, once decided, is imprinted in the soul and manifests itself during life as a deep longing. It is rarely a clear thought, but more often a constant nudging of our silent inner voice. In everyday life, we are constantly making decisions. Our silent voice responds to those decisions, as does the intelligence that permeates nature. When the Afghans say "inshallah" (God-willing) they are referring to this power of God that seems to be ever present, helping us along, pushing us to fulfill our destiny.

If we do not have a clue as to what our destiny is or have become deaf to our inner guide, nature has a way of putting us in circumstances that force us to fulfill our destiny. If we persist in acting against destiny, then everything starts going wrong. There is also a tendency for people in this position to start becoming dishonest. The reason is that when a person starts being dishonest to himself by ignoring his own true impulses, he starts being dishonest to others. Thus the ancient adage: to thine own self be true. To this adage, Shakespeare in *Hamlet* added the line, "And it must follow, as the night the day, thou canst not then be false to any man." The highest loyalty is to that tender voice and to God.

If somehow we manage not to follow our destiny (a very difficult thing, I suppose) then it becomes a "wasted" life. Yet what appears "wasted" may not be so. Many times souls choose great obstacles to develop strength, to burn away impurities in the soul. In these cases, we are not going against destiny; we are bravely embracing it.

A friend once told me that he was sitting with John Lennon one night on a balcony under the stars, talking about spiritual subjects, when Lennon told him that he felt that he was fated to die a violent death. A decade later, he was shot down in New York City. Lennon's character compelled him into music. I doubt if he seriously considered anything else. It is anyone's guess as to why he suffered a violent death. Lennon thought it was his destiny, determined before he was born. I will not second guess him on that.

There is a tendency, especially among men, to identify destiny with profession. This is because men often spend most of their life energy in pursuing and living a career. In a life such as that of Alexander the Great or John Lennon, the career element is prominent. My father dreamed of flying as a child, studied aeronautical engineering in college, flew in the Air Force, and is still flying in his seventies. So that is obviously a major chunk of his destiny. However, career is more properly seen as a medium of destiny, not destiny itself, though this distinction is admittedly fuzzy. A person may be born to be an actress or a lawyer. But it is a medium in which to grow, to pursue the soul's longing, and to influence others in a particular way. Careers come and go, but destiny continues to unfold.

The purpose of destiny is the soul's growth, the chipping away, the forming and polishing of our inner nature. Because we make up a small part of a great web of lives in a society, we also influence the lives of others. So destiny has two sides to it: the growth of our own soul and the influencing of the growth of souls we encounter in everyday living. Selfishness has no place in the larger picture of life, and our destinies are tied to other destinies in such a way as to be mutually beneficial, whether we like it or not. Clearly, some relations do not seem beneficial, but the larger matrix of relations we bounce around in tends to push us all forward.

The only thing in my life that I feel has been compelled and thus amounts to fate is living a spiritual life and sharing it with others. In much of my life, I have avoided sharing my spiritual life with others, trying to hide it and keep it out of sight. But somehow people sense it and try to pull it out of me. I am constantly fighting this, yet slowly losing out to my fate.

But I am viewing my life from a very human point of view. Maybe my life and the life of others is much more destined than I think. Maybe I was "meant" to study law and to throw myself against these larger human problems to force myself to grow and work with others involved in these endeavors. Maybe. Maybe not. Some things remain a mystery.

6

VISIONS

*Disciple: An angel appeared to me robed in
golden light, with eyes of love and
hands of healing, speaking to me in
music of things to come!*

*Master: The future holds a splendor far beyond
what visions or dreams can reveal. Do
not get too attached to them.*

ONE OF MY favorite visions is a recurring one of flying over
mountains—not in an airplane, of course, but like Superman,
though I am never aware of my body. I enjoy it because of
the sense of freedom, the sheer playfulness of flight and
exploration, the lack of care or concern. During one of these
experiences, I saw a white sun rising over the mountains in
the distance. It was a spiritual sun, and I rushed toward it.
During this rush into the sun, I was suddenly grabbed and
taken by a great force to a very different scene: an area of
burned-out buildings, black, devastated, and smoldering.
Then the thought came to me: "nuclear warfare."

The two scenes were opposites. The rising sun symbolized the rise of a spiritual era of peace, and I was irresistibly

drawn to it. The city destroyed by a nuclear explosion symbolized vast turmoil and destruction, and I did not want to see it but was forced to look. My understanding of this vision is that humanity is at the crossroads between an era of spirituality and peace and an era of death and destruction. This is hardly a revelation. The world is at a stage of development where either we get it right or we fall into the whirlpool of chaos.

Or perhaps both are emerging at the same time, vast destruction followed by an era of peace and spirituality. This is the vision of some of the prophets of the new age said to dawn after the year 2000.

In another vision, I saw angelic faces peering down at the world. From their eyes and mouths came a fierce light, like winds of a hurricane, shooting forth to the world below. It was a great transforming energy being put forth to change the world. This also is no revelation. If anything is clear, it is that the world we live in is going through great transformation. We see it all around us. What is less clear is whether there is any rhyme or reason to it. This vision was a moment of clarity of the great spiritual force behind it all, the soul of change. It spoke of resolve and purpose.

Another time, I saw myself standing outside my future home high up on the side of green hills, breathing fresh air. Air is of many types. There is invigorating mountain air, fresh ocean breezes, and the fragrant air of meadows and forests, all rich and full of vitality. But the air I was breathing in this vision was even more special. It was permeated by love, carrying a vibrancy of a much higher nature. What the vision revealed was the inner side of a more evolved society, a future society permeated by love.

For this to evolve, the coarser emotions such as bigotry, hatred, and violence must be purged. This involves great transformation.

The theme of my life has been the dawning of the spiritual sun in my soul. Its light warms me, forcing me to grow and become attuned to its brilliance. It is a common theme. This same sun is dawning within all humanity, warming and forcing great transformation. Universal love is a dawning light emerging within us and spreading across the world. It is a slow process, from the human perspective, and how long it will take to sweep the world is a matter of speculation and prophecy. I am no prophet. But whatever the timetable, its dawning can now be seen as it pushes up against the hard resisting forces of the past.

FROM THE POINT of view of an internationalist, this can be seen in the developments since the end of World War II. Because of the depths of human suffering experienced during World War II, the world responded by giving birth to compassion in the form of international ideals of human rights, a set of standards by which we now measure the worth of societies and governments.

The UN Charter committed the world to human rights, social progress, and world peace, and the Universal Declaration of Human Rights declared that human rights are "inherent" in people and form the foundation for "freedom, justice, and peace in the world." Overnight, these latent seeds sprouted from the minds of philosophers and poets to become formal legal instruments affirmed by the nations of the world. The existence of such documents is significant because it gives direction to global development. It also represents the underlying spiritual life breaking forth in humanity.

The execution of these ideals is another matter. Although slow and cumbersome, there has been a global march of democratization sweeping through Latin America, Asia, Africa, eastern Europe, and the former Soviet Union.

Global democratization is slowly moving toward, for a lack of a better term, world federalism. This century has witnessed two apparently opposing developments. One has been the growth of unity among nations through a vast web of international treaties resulting in, among other things, the UN, the European Union, the WTO, ASEAN, and NAFTA. The other has been the separation of nations by the rise of local autonomy and self-determination movements.

The separation movements were most evident in the decolonization of Africa and Asia, the fall of the Soviet Union, and the breakup of Yugoslavia. Less evident but more prevalent has been the growing power of autonomy among provinces and other local areas inside nations. Scotland, for example is beginning to develop its own political identity. This phenomena is sweeping the world, emerging in China, India, Europe, and the Americas.

These two developments, global integration and separatist movements, are caused by a single underlying force: the need for a "vertical" balance in the cascade of political powers from the smallest village to the UN. At the end of World War II, the nation-state was the single most powerful political entity, but the nation-state was inadequate in governing the local affairs of villages and towns far removed from the concerns of centralized governments. The nation-states were also inadequate in managing global affairs, as the world wars demonstrated. These two political areas, global affairs and local affairs, needed to develop and the power of the nation-state slowly eroded as power shifted internally to local governments and externally to international organizations.

Political union is an outer expression of the inner development of love. Political union does not mean the loss of identity, but the harmony of differences by sharing common ideals. It is the diversity of culture and traditions that give life its color and provides the dynamics by which humans learn from each other. This is why I tell the Tibetans that there is no need to separate from China. All that is needed is to become involved in the democratization of China, and the growth of local autonomy will give them more freedom than they can ever imagine, while enjoying the economic and cultural benefits of association with China.

My vision of world federalism in its full flowering will have little resemblance to today's world. It will be a global village in which people are united spiritually by shared ideals and are united physically by advanced technologies in travel and communication. The nation-states will be marginalized or will disappear completely in the web of communities from small villages to towns, cities, provinces, regional unions, and world bodies. As an individual's freedom is protected by civil rights, so will the freedoms of cities, provinces, and other political entities be protected by autonomy rights. The world government would thus stand at the political pinnacle as a very limited, but clearly defined, power designed to harmonize (not oppress) the diversity of global culture. Hunger, epidemics, and war will fade out. I do not think human problems will disappear, but they will be on a different level, representing different challenges.

The theme of the new era of peace will be love. I am not talking about people walking around with silly smiles on their faces all the time. I am talking about a humanity permeated by a higher, finer energy, characterized best by the qualities of love, peace, and joy. Physicians will be healers who attend to the whole person, not just the body. The spiritual energy flowing from them will have a direct healing influence, soothing the patient's soul as well as infusing life-energy into the body. Science will become spiritual, integrating morality and God into the big picture.

The changing political landscape will adopt itself to reflect the flowering of the human spirit. Politics will finally overcome the influence of money and media. High technology and the emergence of clairvoyance will make secrets impossible and the true nature of politicians known to all. Political decision-making will be shared by a much wider section of the populace, possibly by greater use of the initiative and referendum through the Internet. Communities will become smaller, surrounded and permeated by the beauty of nature. Yet they will be more integrated with the world through high technology than today's most sophisticated cities. Energy sources will be wireless, no longer dependent on oil, and environmentally pure. And vehicles will be artificially "intelligent" so as to make accidents a thing of the past.

FROM A COSMIC point of view, I imagine there is a certain inevitability in the unfolding of a new era. But there is also a margin in which humanity may help the process along or resist and hinder it. Innumerable decisions will be made that will affect people's lives in either a positive or negative manner.

In the introduction, I offered two suggestions to help things along: more involvement of the private sector in global transformation, and the need for spiritual regeneration. I reiterate that it is the people's world, and people should be progressively more involved in business, the arts, education, and the world of NGOs in pushing and pulling things along. We cannot depend exclusively on governments.

One idea for helping the process along through spiritual regeneration is to have large gatherings of people from all spiritual or religious traditions in the world for the purpose of worshipping God together as one human family.

There is a tendency for people to see thoughts as a phantom event occurring within the skull. But thoughts have a force and energy that project outward to the world like a radiance. When someone embraces us in love, our soul is warmed by that love much in the same way that sunshine warms the body. It is an energy that penetrates and caresses. When a child gets up on stage and experiences stage fright, it is often because she is experiencing the many thoughts directed at her. She is not accustomed to that energy. When a person shouts obscenities or otherwise speaks condescendingly and rudely, it is an energy that penetrates us with its ugliness. A strong personality is little affected by such attacks, but a person in a moment of vulnerability may be crushed by it. War cries and black magic are the most negative expression of this.

Thoughts can coalesce to form a collective reality, like small streams coming together to form a raging river. The thoughts of hate and oppression among the fundamentalist

Taliban coalesced to form a great destructive force, as did the collective thoughts of the Nazis, Khmer Rouge, and other dark forces in human history. In contrast, people who come together with common thoughts of love send out a great tidal wave of positive energy into the world. Those who walk into such a gathering can feel the energy, and the world around the gathering is inevitably influenced by it.

In India there is a concept called *darshan*. When they say in India, that "I got a darshan from a yogi," they are saying that they sat in the radiance of the yogi's being. I have noticed this over the years with the holy people I have met. There is a soothing, calming, and often joyful energy that is radiated. It is not from their thoughts, but from their being, which is infused with love and wisdom; it is infused with a energy that has trickled down from the divine. We all radiate a certain form of this energy. A gathering of spiritually minded people would radiate a massive wave of spiritual energy.

Such a gathering would include a conference of prayers, meditations, chanting, pujas, ceremonies, and a lot of spiritually oriented music and discussions. I am talking of thousands of people gathering together at one time and doing so periodically every six months to a year in different parts of the world.

The emphasis would not be on doctrine, but on the spiritual experience, which the gathering would radiate to the world. Doctrines vary greatly, but the underlying spiritual experience is universal. It would be a gathering of humanity reaching up together to the highest heavens, pulling some of the world with it. The high spiritual energy generated would seep into the world, soothing it and providing a healing balm and inspiration. Such gatherings would help to pull the world to its spiritual destiny. The degree of impact is not clear to me. But clearly there would be some impact that would make it worth the effort.

I CANNOT IMAGINE an end to the growth of the human soul. But I can imagine a type of mastery of human society somewhere in the far distant future. Imagine humanity as a long stream of spiritual evolution. Presently, we see ourselves as separate from each other. In areas of the world where physical and emotional violence prevail, the separateness is acutely exaggerated. Now imagine a progression of spiritual evolution where we become more and more aware of our common source of spiritual life. The walls of separateness begin to break down. At some point what will predominate will be our union, not our separateness.

Imagine a great crystal with billions of facets, each shining with an inner light. Each facet shares the same inner light from the center of this great crystal, yet each facet is different, refracting a different aspect of this light. This is how I see a fully formed humanity. Like the many facets on the crystal, each of us becomes fully rooted in the same spiritual source of eternal Spirit, yet each remains distinctly individual. Here, humanity will find its highest and purest peace.

INDEX

D

E

F

W

Y

Z

ABOUT THE AUTHOR

Roger Plunk was born into a military family, growing up while living in various places and fostering his habit of roaming. He holds law degrees from Florida State University and George Washington University, and worked at the U.S. State Department before an invitation from the Dalai Lama's administration set him out on the journeys described in *The Wandering Peacemaker*. He currently resides in Iowa, but is quick to say that his only home is his website. *The Wandering Peacemaker* is his first book.

Hampton Roads Publishing Company

. . . for the evolving human spirit

Hampton Roads Publishing Company
publishes books on a variety of subjects including
metaphysics, health, complementary medicine,
visionary fiction, and other related topics.

For a copy of our latest catalog,
call toll-free, 800-766-8009,
or send your name and address to:

Hampton Roads Publishing Company, Inc.
1125 Stoney Ridge Road
Charlottesville, VA 22902
e-mail: hrpc@hrpub.com
www.hrpub.com